The New Shape

of American Religion

Christianity is not concerned with religion;

it is concerned with Jesus Christ.

—PETER L. BERGER, PARAPHRASING DIETRICH BONHOEFFER

The New Shape
of American Religion

by Martin E. Marty

Harper & Brothers
Publishers, New York

To My Parents

Contents

Preface

THIS BOOK is a call for a culture ethic for American Protestantism. It includes an analysis of the new shape of American
religion against the background of the past. Its second portion is
devoted to resources and strategy for reshaping Protestantism in a
new cultural situation. This includes a full-length illustration from
the example of the Christian parish. Viewed from this aspect, the
book is to be seen as a preliminary contribution to parochial
theology. Finally, the spirit of revitalized Protestant witness is
discussed.

As a preliminary study this is submitted in the knowledge that
others have been articulate on this subject (and my debt to many
of them is patent on these pages) and that still others must be
called to participate out of their varying vocations. As such a culture ethic matures, I believe that it can do for America's current
cultural discontents what the Social Gospel achieved in an earlier
social crisis. What is more, it can learn from the mistakes of that
movement.

The idea for such an effort grew out of conversations with
Franklin Sherman of the State University of Iowa who expressed
interest in a "Social Gospel of Culture" and with William H. Kirkland of Vanderbilt University who has since apocopated the phrase
and given it clarity in his term, "Needed: A Culture Ethic."

The discussion of "the new shape of American religion" involves
me in a risky approach to a *Gestalt,* a whole, that seems to presup-
pose an American consensus and a homogeneity of experience

which the variety of American life often denies. American religion looks vastly different from within a ghetto, a great city, or the Bible Belt. While seeking to do justice to the exceptions, I believe we can with some confidence summarize and generalize our emerging national experiment, and these hazards become necessary as part of "interim reports." This then is current history written from the viewpoint expressed by Abraham Lincoln in 1858: "If we could first know where we are, and whither we are tending, we could better judge what to do, and how to do it."

I am grateful to The Christian Century Foundation and to Dr. Harold Fey for permission to reprint the portions of this manuscript which originally appeared in *The Christian Century* and to my colleagues there who shared in its production. Particularly, I thank Cecelia Gaul for translating my manuscript into English prose and to Fern Koelling for typing it. The discussion of the poise of the parish is indebted to the men who nudged me into and along the way in a pastoral ministry, particularly William F. Bruening, the late Louis J. Sieck, and Otto A. Geiseman. Finally, my family was patient in those days of last summer's "vacation" and the hours of early morning and late night when the book was being written, and I thank them. While much of the book is of a critical character, I offer it with a great sense of involvement in, and love for, Protestantism in America and to the Lord to which it is committed.

MARTIN E. MARTY

Chicago, Illinois
Good Friday, 1959

The New Shape

of American Religion

Introduction

Erosion: The Shaping of
the New American Religious Scene

T HE NEW shape of American religion is the result of the erosion and corrosion worked in by the American environment on the religions which have thrived in it. The variety of creeds, the competition through the long years among denominations, the experimental spirit, and the necessities of accommodation have served as eroding agents. Religions have always engaged in dialogue with their environment. A hostile milieu erodes religious particularity least of all: oppressed groups become insular and protect themselves. The setting which American experience presented was attractive to religious groups, but it left them in exposed positions. The churches' reply was at once defensive and aggressive: If religion was to be Americanized, America should be religionized.

So it is that a nation which made no legal provision for maintaining and supporting religion has become more religious than most nations having a religious establishment. The great majority of us prefer this result to most of its alternatives. We generally take for granted the congeniality of our nation to the various faiths; but when we pause to reflect we are awed.

Religion in America has paid a price for its accommodation to an environment which religionists often regarded as being somehow revelatory and redemptive. I will argue that the price has been paid thoughtlessly and unnecessarily. Considering the turn of events in the middle of the twentieth century, it would appear that

1

the best interests neither of America nor of the particular religions are being served through continued payment.

We have been seeing the maturing of several processes: the erosion of particularity, the smoothing of the edges of witness, the loss of religious content. Particularity is challenged by a blurry, generalizing religion; distinctive witness is confronted by amiable syncretism; theological content is often replaced by sentiments about religion. The process of erosion has been long and gradual and its full effect has only recently become noticeable. It is now working so rapidly to change the religious setting of America that predicting the future would be highly hazardous. We shall tiptoe to the edge of that future, and leave the argument there. Mainstream religion in America can still go either of two ways: it can allow itself to be further eroded; or, through the responsible witnesses to the activity of God, it can build dikes and levees and plant shelter belts of trees against the eroding winds and waters.

Much of my argument will be directed primarily to contemporary Protestantism. But even were it restricted to this audience its destiny should not be too limited. According to the churches' rolls, America now has over 60,000,000 Protestants; and according to some surveys, about 80,000,000 people over the age of fourteen think of themselves as Protestant. A study directed to this American minority could hardly be considered esoteric. But I have a larger end also in view. Most of the concerns expressed for Protestantism can, by simple translation, be applied to Roman Catholicism and Judaism. I have seldom paused to undertake the translation because it would confuse the direction of my argument. Moreover, Protestantism has the larger investment in the American past and the most at stake in the American present. It seems hardly necessary to document this obvious fact. But several reminders are in order.

America was once largely Protestant—just *how* Protestant should be clear to anyone who examines the statistical picture of the past, Protestantism's effects both bad and good on our national institutions, or the alternate boasting and complaining of the historians of Protestantism's competitors for the American's mind and heart. The American religious past is best described by pointing out what it was not.

It was, first of all, not Jewish. Judaism has been represented here for three centuries and the several million Jews in the country today have an influence far beyond their numbers, but even a cursory glance at the past will show that Jewish influence then was of a minority character. Historians of Judaism must strain when they attempt to fuse its history with the broader national experience, and apologists for Jewry need not range far afield to document the effects of Old World anti-Semitism in America. The goaders of Judaism still complain of the overlong shadow of the ghetto which followed their people to the New World.

Nor was America in the main Roman Catholic. When the nation was born there were probably no more than 25,000 Catholics in a population of four million. By 1900 there were over 12,000,000 Catholics, but much of this represented isolated "foreign" colonies in certain cities. Only since 1910 or thereabouts has Roman Catholicism taken its place as a new virtual majority (though still a statistical minority) in American life. Today, according to historian John Tracy Ellis, the actual Catholic population is probably nearer 40,000,000 than 33,574,017, the figure given by the *Official Catholic Directory* for 1956.

From the founders of Maryland through the Carroll family of Baltimore down to modern civic leaders, Roman Catholics have played a significant role in shaping American institutions and culture. But the special pleading of Catholicism's apologists becomes embarrassing whenever too large a role is claimed for Catholic influence in America's early days. And this pleading is constantly being drowned out by Catholic complainants of persecution at the hands of the Protestant majority. Similarly, Catholic realists urge their brethren not to try to pre-empt the Protestant past but to see themselves and their mission today in the light of eighteenth- and nineteenth-century experiences which were not their own.

Protestant historians used to enjoy suggesting that God in His Providence had hidden the New World from the eyes of men until the Reformation of the sixteenth century. This pious notion did little to explain why the United States should have been favored over most of the rest of North America or how it happened that all of South America slipped through the fingers of Providence. But there was an element of truth in their observation that it was in America that Protestantism, for all its schisms, first had the opportunity—to which Protestants were often forced and dragged —to put Protestant principles into positive fact.

They liked to tell of Francis Higginson, one of the first two Puritan ministers to arrive in Massachusetts, and to quote the speech he is reported to have made on shipboard as England was lost from sight:

> We will not say as the separatists were wont to say at their leaving England, "Farewell, Babylon! Farewell, Rome!" but we will say, "Fare- wel, dear England, Farewel the Church of God in England and all the Christian friends there!" We do not go to New England as Separatists from the Church of England, though we cannot but separate from the corruptions in it; but we go to practice the positive part of church reformation, and propagate the gospel in America.

This may well belong in the "remarks we doubt ever got re- marked" columns, but a host of Higginson's successors would have defined their mission similarly. *They came to practice the positive part of church reformation and to propagate the Gospel.* America was a Zion, its cliffsides not yet eroded; it was a city set upon a hill, whose slopes the streams had not yet worn away. America was to be a great Protestant empire.

Insofar as organized religion was represented in the great central events that shaped America and have become part of its mystic inner core, Protestantism dominated. Most of the permanent colonization of the original states was done by Protestants; many of the contributors (by necessity or by choice) to religious freedom were Protestants; the westward movement and the propagation of the Gospel on the frontier were largely led by Protestants.

But through it all, Protestantism was not alone. More and more it shared its status with Roman Catholicism and Judaism. All along it shared its position with a sort of casually Deist natural religion, an attitude toward life and religion which was informed by the Enlightenment. This attitude never became an organized religious movement in America because it did not need to. Most of the founding fathers and most of the adherents of the major religions held to its presuppositions. But this attitude is coming to new maturity in the middle of the twentieth century, and I shall devote considerable attention to its corrosive influences. For three centuries then, America's religious pluralism, coupled with the competition among faiths, the capitulations of Protestants, the pressures of environmental change, and a fundamentally generalizing attitude toward religion, have worked to erode Protestant particularity and to wear down the walls of the Zion which had symbolized Protestantism's status.

If this is so, there are reasons for concern on the part of those of us who feel that Higginson's statement of purpose was valid and is still largely unfulfilled. The task of practicing the positive part of church reformation and propagating the Gospel in America is complicated by its new setting. What follows is a story about this new setting.

One

The Revival of Interest in Religion

THE PROCESS of erosion of religion by the American environment was remarkably accelerated by the revival of interest in religion which began during World War II. Since it was this revival that helped bring about the new shape of American religion, we shall spend some time in an effort to determine its real character. Neither the religious awakening itself nor the simple erosion of meaningful religious distinctions attendant thereon was a new phenomenon in mid-twentieth-century America. Both appeared against and out of a complex historical pattern. The present manifestation will make sense only if we look at it in the context of revivals that went before.

Most of us have come to think of the rhythmic movement, the pendulous pattern of response in American religion, as normative for all religious activity. Indeed, the fact that the spiritual impulse seems to ebb and flow in nations and times and seasons as it must in individuals, should be documentable. The historian of the twenty Christian centuries, however, is inclined to view these surges from the longer perspective, marking them only over the long stride of the decades. It was in America, where religion was free of the state and dependent on its own resources, that men first found it possible to date the changes in tempo by the annual calendar if not the hourglass. The pace of American life, the developing ease of communication, the fascination of a nation with a thriving (and

6

unsubsidized) constellation of churches—all bred curiosity. We have always wanted to know "how things are going" between God and man. We do not want to wait for the historians ten or fifty years hence to summarize a time of revival; we want them to clock it with a stop watch and measure its fervor with a thermometer.

So it was that toward the end of every religious awakening on American soil—at least according to its historians of later times—there grew a restiveness to analyze its meaning. Oddly, whenever our fathers were conscious of being in the midst of a revival, it seemed to be slipping away. The pattern, discussed by the conventional chronicles, is almost wearyingly familiar. After a time of apathy or disaffection a new spirit breaks forth in the land, concomitant with the appearance of some gifted or even charismatic preacher (or preachers) of the Good News, who stirs hearts and provides headlines. Usually the preacher is itinerant, making an impression at many points on a map. After a time the spirit is spent, and stifling a yawn the nation settles back into its earlier apathy. Ordinarily, the churches chart statistical gains and bask in national favor just at the time they must steel themselves for the long hard winter of nonrevival which they assume must follow as night follows day.

Whether we do well to accept such a stereotype is not the question here; the fact is that most of us do accept it. But the present revival has brought with it some highly novel features which do not conform to the pattern of the past. For one thing, as a nation we are reaching a point of near-saturation so far as religious interest goes. And the religion involved is largely so inoffensive that the pendulum of reaction is not likely to swing far. In other words, the current revival, while extensive, in many of its aspects lacks depth. There has been less investment; there need be less withdrawal. For this is that utterly new thing: a revival that goes not against the grain of the nation but with it; a revival that draws its strength from its safe residence in the mores of the nation. Hence it has proved largely invulnerable to the assaults of critics outside the churches. America is religionized. It has been on a religious "kick" and does not wish to be bothered. When on occasion the cultured despisers of religion or the latter-day muckrakers have spoken up they have found themselves frustrated and bewildered. They were not stoned, as blasphemers once were—and this is not simply because people nowadays are more civil and genteel than their forefathers were, but because they did not know what the critics were talking about. In short, critics of past revivals might be attacking God. Critics of this one have had to tangle with something much more protected and less vulnerable: religion made secure in the national ethos, custom, and favor. So it devolved on men from within the churches to raise the necessary questions.

Let us look at the present thrust for God in the context of six previous and specifically Christian conversion campaigns. Against that background the dramatic difference between the current stir and its predecessors should stand out most clearly. We are to ask in what ways erosion of valid distinctions in religion were accelerated by the newest revival, and why. There has, of course, always been erosion, and in part it has been caused by pragmatic considerations. To promote religious response men have often found it necessary to unite on many grounds while seeming to gloss over separating factors.

The First Great Awakening in America occurred in the 1730s and is associated with the names of Jonathan Edwards and George Whitefield. It extended from New England to New Jersey and aroused the comatose Protestantism that had flourished [sic] in colonial times. Few events in American history did more to erode the Calvinistic theology which Edwards enunciated with such precision than did the revival that is to this day symbolized by his name. The Second Great Awakening—as clearly identifiable as its predecessor in the accounts of historians—came around 1801. It was a reaction to the rationalism and post-Revolutionary period of indifference to religion. The awakeners in New England were reasonably sophisticated proponents of a softened Edwardsianism; yet they found common cause with the very different evangelizers on the frontier. And it was the theology and practice of these ruder Arminians that came to characterize the decade.

The third, larger revival coincided with the decades-long conquest of the frontier for evangelicalism under Lyman Beecher, Peter Cartwright, and their kin and kind. In this period a sense of common evangelicalism developed in America. In the name of "winning America for God" men of many denominations found it necessary and possible to settle a variety of unsettled and unsettling differences which the luxury of another age had indulged. Few had time to think. When this activity had spent itself, an urban reaction to religious indifference among laymen came to prominence. That fourth revival was in the year 1858. The Y.M.C.A. in America is a monument to this prayer-centered movement of benevolence. One great assumption behind this movement was that good men of good will can come together to nudge a nation nearer to God despite the irrelevant differences in their theologies. Let the professors in academies and seminaries worry their heads over those.

By the time Dwight L. Moody and his colleagues and cohorts assembled a new band of fidelity to march out against infidelity (a fifth "awakening"), all this blurring had come to pass *within* evangelical Protestantism. Now a new foil presented itself. A liberal Christianity had appeared and seemed to be making concessions to the new age, adapting itself too compromisingly to the world of Darwin and Spencer. Moody and his men would have no truck with such accommodation. They represented conservatism and orthodoxy. Yet, curiously, they too contributed largely to the fuzzying of differences by their reduction of the complexities of Christianity to a "simple Gospel" which shoe clerks and dishwashers could understand. And which the intellectualist liberal Christians could not. The sixth phase, in the twentieth century, saw Billy Sunday and his last-gasp "old time revivalism" adding to this mixture little that was new except noise.

What is marked from Edwards down to Billy Sunday (and I use the word "down" advisedly) is the way the more conservative side of mainstream Protestant Christianity—the side that was always most effected by revival—saw its particular witness erode against the environment or corrode as it contacted somewhat different witnesses. To say this is not to pronounce a judgment. As a matter of fact, much of this intraevangelical smoothing out of edges may very well have been the most salutary single by-product of revivalism. The concern of well-meaning men for common causes often brought them nearer to one another, and the ecumenical movement of the twentieth century is in many respects the grandchild of the evangelical movement of the nineteenth. The eroding principle became dangerous only when a completely new element was introduced into the revival pattern. That "something new" first appeared in the 1950s.

Having run my rake over as much of the reporting on *this* revival as possible, I am most impressed by the neglect of what seems to me the most important aspect of it. Since World War II we have been witnessing the first great awakening not of mainstream Protestant Christianity as such but *of a maturing national religion.* This is clear if we examine the six previous impulses as they are forged in our folklore and lauded by our minstrels: in none of them were Roman Catholicism, Judaism, and secular humanism, or any one of the three, appreciably involved. Indeed, they were often in varying degrees the evil foe, the bogey that would stir evangelicals to crusade for God.

The revival of the 1950s saw a great change in this respect. The faiths, Christian or not, which would conspire to religionize America on a mass scale were nearly equally involved, and all were experiencing gains from the interest of those years. But the initiative for revival came not so much from an outburst of prophetic preaching with a Biblical orientation, a proclamation designed to bring a nation to its knees. Instead, this new initiative came from the spirit of the times and the cultural acceptability of religious faith. Thus President Dwight D. Eisenhower's pastor reminded the nation that it should be grateful that the President's deeply felt faith made religious interest manly once again. The nation already knew this. Protestants, Catholics, and Jews were exceptionally responsive—give them credit for alertness to the times—and the majority in each group was ready to climb on the rolling revival's band wagon, without even asking the price of the ticket.

This amounted to even more than an awakening of the three (or four) great faiths. If we read the banner on the band wagon that swept the 1950s we shall see that it represented a revival of *interest* in religion. "Interest" is a rather limp and noncommittal word to be using about discussion of ultimates. It carries overtones of self-advantage and self-concern more than other-advantage and God-concern. It need imply little more than curiosity. Yet "interest" is the term characteristically used both casually by neutral observers or deliberately by men who are trying to make a point. One of these latter was C. S. Lewis, writing in *Punch* (July 9, 1958) in reply to a fictitious questioner who asked whether Lewis would "deny that there is . . . a great, even growing interest in religion?" The answer:

I suppose there is a fairly widespread interest. But I don't feel sure [the questioner] is interpreting it correctly. In the days when most people had a religion, what he meant by "an interest in religion" could hardly have existed. For of course religious people—that is, people when they are being religious—are not "interested in religion." Men who have gods worship those gods; it is the spectators who describe this as "interest in religion." . . . The moment a man seriously accepts a deity his interest in "religion" is at an end. He's got something else to think about. The ease with which we can now get an audience for a discussion of religion does not prove that people are becoming more religious. What it really proves is the existence of a large "floating vote."

This could be a "text for the sermon." How the floating vote was cast in America in the 1950s can now be examined with a measure of dispassion and a bit of perspective. We can begin to grasp at the whole of what was happening while we were all interested spectators. In the form in which it was born, the revival seemed to have crested toward the end of the decade. Whether new impulses will stir or not is for the cult of foretellers to predict. At any rate that a change of pace occurred is not surprising. The word "revival" carries with it a tone of the transitory. To affirm that a resurgence is here is to be aware also that it may go.

Signs of the beginning of the end appeared in 1957, and the downward pace accelerated thereafter. First of the signs was the spate of questioning magazine articles and books on the subject. One of the earliest was William Peters' story in *Redbook* (November 1957), "The Growing Doubts about Our Religious Revival." A little later A. Roy Eckardt could write in *The Surge of Piety in America:* "There are, indeed, some signs that the crest of the recent flood of religious interest may already have passed. At this writing, the new piety is becoming a little old. It is not quite so vocal or manifest as it was as recently as one or two years ago."[1]

Why these signs of tiring? First, because the original energies had largely been spent. The cast of the revival was set in the late 1940s and the early 1950s. A new moderate political regime found religious alliance congenial. Television and paperback books opened new doors to a massive broadcast of religious tenets. A number of individuals independently discovered the power of religion in the face of anxiety and in the quest for personal success. The personality cult produced a new kind of success saint. Christians found ways of reviving mass revivalism.

These crests, were they to be charted chronologically across the face of the 1950s, would resemble overlapping parabolas. Between 1951 and 1954 the religion of political fanaticism reached its peak with McCarthyism. We can hardly now recapture the smells of incense and sulphur that met each other then as theistic democracy fought atheistic Communism. Political piety was in vogue up to and shortly after the presidential election of 1952, after which it declined somewhat. Whether renewed cold-war tensions or the mystic chords of memory stirred by the centennial of the Civil War will reawaken this piety remains to be seen.

The crest came later for those proponents of faith who had reached a large public via television or best-selling books. Reading Eckardt's book, printed in 1958, one is impressed to observe how dated are the replies to Norman Vincent Peale. Criticism of that stripe has diminished. Even the great Peter Marshall could hardly survive the blasphemy of the movie advertisements touting his virtues posthumously. An *Esquire* cartoon matter-of-factly named 1955 the peak year of the intellectuals' fascination with religion; the date is probably exact enough. Billy Graham's finest hour came in 1957 in New York; the rest is repetition. David had met Goliath and as Eckardt says, "Goliath yawned." So did other Philistines.

This brings us to the second manifestation of change. There were signs of surfeit among the people, signs that they had heeded the old Gospel song and taken "time to be holy," and were back in business as usual.

> For as a surfeit of the sweetest things
> The deepest loathing to the stomach brings,
> Or as the heresies that men do leave
> Are hated most of those they did deceive. . . .

Recognizing this to be so, concerned churchmen tried to capture and make use of the moment after satiety had set in. The reports on church affiliation during 1957 recorded a marked drop in gains as against the gain in national population. The Chicago Church Federation was reluctant to support Billy Graham. As a nation we were second into space and this failure to outstrip the Russians brought new insecurities. After our President and Secretary of State had given all those assurances about God's dependence on us, was not this a betrayal? Why be holy, if that was how it paid? Churches, sensing the moment, began to revise their work lest they lose the gains of the decade. Not that they expected a violent repudiation of religion. America in its newly religionized state was not likely to react violently. It would simply take religion for granted instead of mocking (or practicing?) it.

Third, and most of all, the later 1950s proved a wedge for the return of reaction, however gently. The President was relegated to merely human status by the press which had once glorified him. John Foster Dulles, once praised for Christian statesmanship, was criticized for shallow moralizing even in his hours of personal crisis. "Beatniks" drew attention to themselves despite their minor talents because the nation was ready for some mark of change. The no-religion of Zen Buddhism developed its cult. The loudest burp from a satiated nation came in the happily short-lived round of "sick jokes" that had their blasphemous hour. The pseudo-religious cult of togetherness was regularly chided and nonreligious nonconformity was presented as an image and an ideal in some circles. The outspoken Harry Golden said damning things about the impotence and apathy of the churches in his bestseller and in national magazines, and none dared contradict him. Bertrand Russell and Julian Huxley reappeared on publishers' lists. A philosophy major at Harvard broke a lance on Memorial Church and shook that urbane citadel of symbolic intellectual return to religion. *Harper's* could print "The Faith of a Heretic" and *The Nation,* "A Pagan Sermon to the Christian Clergy."

Within two years the change had come. Where a short time before it would have been extremely difficult to compile a list of signs of satiety, now one could not conclude it easily.

If the revival as we knew it was coming to some sort of end we could be assured of one enduring result: the erosion of religious particularity it had occasioned. Were we to make a list of manifestations which profited most (or least) by the revival, it might look something like this:

> *Interest in religion* was dominant.
> *The New American Religion* had found assured status.
> *Protestantism-Catholicism-Judaism* were prosperous.
> *Evangelical Protestantism* was tumbled from its past prominence on the revivals' scales.

For their seats on the band wagon, the four phenomena might be pictured in opposite order:

> *Evangelical Protestantism* suffered most by erosion.
> *Protestantism-Catholicism-Judaism* were somewhat vulnerable because of their uncritical acceptance of alien norms.
> *The New American Religion* was safely embedded in the mores.
> *Interest in religion* might come and go at will: it was respectable and secure.

It is the task of evangelical Christianity, in keeping with the revelation to which it witnesses, to be critical of "interest in religion" as such. Interest in religion seems so obviously preferable to indifference, and the religious vogue so preferable to antireligion, that many have been bewildered at the efforts of those who would flash caution lights before the rolling band wagon. Show critics a nation heaven-bent on salvation—what more could they want? Yet in the name of Biblical religion they express indifference and occasional dismay—why? To answer these questions it will be necessary to explore several aspects of the erosive impulse and to analyze enduring assets of Biblical religion. Let us first look at the revival in more detail. What was it all about?

The nation had become newly interested in religion after the disaffection of the 1930s, a time of economic depression. The new interest gained momentum during World War II: "There are no atheists in foxholes." Immediately after the war it declined somewhat, but in the late 1940s a great change began. Suddenly new records for church attendance were being set. More and more Americans became part of organized church life. The denominations looked at the tabulations on their electronic adding machines and were awed at their own successes. These statistics would give most experts a queasy feeling because of their patent inaccuracies, but we cannot fail to be impressed by the upward swing. Note the record of percentages of "church members" in America over several years:

1920:	43.0%
1930:	47.0%
1940:	49.0%
1950:	57.0%
1954:	60.3%
1955:	60.9%
1956:	62.0%

When pollsters walked by with questions concerning belief in God virtually everyone affirmed that he held such belief. For the first time in decades religious books again became bestsellers and movie makers saw the need for inserting God into their bubble-bath productions. Civic organizations found it necessary to incorporate religion into their activities. The businessmen's prayer rooms belong to the architecture of this era. Where religious symbolism failed, national images formed the iconostasis. George Washington (kneeling) appeared in stained glass in the famed prayer room in Washington. Even the United Nations as it head-quartered in America had to provide a meditation room which most Americans assumed was to be used for prayer. "In God We Trust" had to be stamped also on the folding symbols of America's bow to Mammon. (Fortunately, *which* God was not specified.) Citizens learned to pledge loyalty not simply under the flag but also under God, no matter what it did to the rhythms of the little liturgy of the public schools. The popular music market picked up the gospel beat.

And more. Church building became the fourth largest private building category as citizens erected tangible symbols of their devotion. Some intellectuals found religion respectable once again, and religious propaganda directed to the disaffected urban areas found some response among the lower classes. But the real strength of the revival came from the middle-brow middle class, the New Americans who seemed to congregate in the suburbs. At the center of these impulses was what the late Paul Hutchinson called the "cult of reassurance"—"a sort of alliance between one aspect of religion, the 'I will fear no evil' aspect, and depth psychology to overcome modern personality disintegrations." All this was best symbolized by the familiar tale of the actress who confided to a friend that she always consulted her horoscope. Friend: "I didn't know you believe in astrology!" "Oh, yes, I believe in everything—a little bit."

In place of worship or service or thought, one aspect of character was stressed: *sincerity*. It did not matter what one believed, be he Protestant, Catholic, Jew, Orthodox, Inventor of Religion, Cultist—as long as he was sincere. Many people forgot that Mao Tse-tung, Khrushchev, and Franco may also have been sincere. The sincerity that was admired was the marketable type. It seemed attainable by all. When the image was frequently tarnished as in the case of "sincere" motion picture stars, the manufacturers of the image could polish a new one. The appeal of sincerity seemed to inhere in that it was an understandable virtue. It was not remote, the way saintliness is. It was not profound, the way sacrifice was. It was a quality with which everyone could identify himself or herself. Though possibly out of reach of some, it was only just barely out of reach. With a little effort it could belong to anyone. What more was expected?

When we translate all these feelings and phenomena from individual experience to their social effects, the psychosocial bases of this revival of interest are patent. At the risk of making myself vulnerable to the charge of not allowing room for the winds of the Holy Spirit to blow, to stir, to inspire, to fire, we shall examine one approach to these social notes.

Can we not assume the continued work of the Spirit and still point to the manifestations that are open to observation? In the 1950s, just as often before in times of anxiety and dislocation, men were compelled to the search for meaning and security. In addition to this failure of nerve a variety of social causes is cited. Perhaps Milton J. Rosenberg's analysis is touched with cynicism, but one cannot argue with most of what he said in an article in *Pastoral Psychology* in June 1957: "However else one may wish to approach it, the religious revival is a social phenomenon of high visibility. As such it requires a social explanation: that is, an explanation which will relate it to the psychological processes of individual man and the social order or disorder in which he is situated." Rosenberg was dissatisfied with the limited "failure of nerve" hypothesis, and his instincts were probably correct.

First, the "elevation of conformity" was highly visible. When the United States was faced by a threat from without and plagued by inner doubts it tended to demand and mobilize high degrees of consensus in thought and then in patterns of life. Seen in this light, much of the renewed interest in religion amounted to "playing it safe." Second, the huckster was uncommonly successful. Mass media came into their own in this period. The advances in advertising and in the development of television as a medium of persuasion account for much. According to Rosenberg, Madison Avenue, the symbol of huckstering, in its advocacy of religion was out to justify itself to itself. In his irreverent paraphrase: "Luce does more than Niebuhr can to justify God's ways to man."

These two factors in the revival are so obvious that they should be mistrusted if we think of them as exhaustive. So Professor Rosenberg of Yale went on to ask in what ways the revival satisfied lasting and real human needs. Here a third factor, the more profound quest for community came into play. In a time of disruption and isolation and brokenness, religion—both good and bad religion—offered some kind of community. The nation's joiners had not found satisfaction themselves by joining secular associations. "We hunger for a kind of group association in which, through being ourselves, we may get to something greater than ourselves. We long to touch the transcendent and, furthermore, to do it in the company of others who, by sharing our experiences, verify and confirm them."

Those among the laity and the clergy who guide our religious institutions and govern our churches seem to have become aware that people are coming to church not simply to partake of the sacred but to partake of sacred *community*. The result is that today through broad programs of social events and organizational campaigns many of our churches are providing their communicants with the pleasures of *sacred* gregariousness which serves ego-enhancement much better than *mere* gregariousness or selfish gregariousness.

Here we might all raise some questions and point to the other side of the same argument. Professor Rosenberg did not mention that people are coming to church to partake of *sacred* community! Many who wish to remain nameless and who are untouched by gregariousness find resource in worship. But for the truth that is involved in Rosenberg's half-truth we do well to follow his argument.

Particularly in a time of community disruption caused by mobility there was need for routinized sociability on a transgeographical level (Rosenberg's terms). As people "carry their church memberships with them from Long Island to the San Fernando Valley they carry with them a continuity of community made possible largely by this very commitment to organized religion."

A fourth visible factor was the cultural discrepancy between ethic and practice: "While the Judeo-Christian forms are being resuscitated their content has already been seriously altered. Religious man is very busy these days justifying his ways to God." Here Rosenberg scored the Peales and the Liebmans who recast God as psychiatrist and promised that which lay beyond their province to promise. The popular religionists have rewritten the religious vision to give "sacred sanction to a way of life that we have been forced into and must somehow make morally legitimate."

Instead of arguing with detail here I shall set down certain cautions by reminding that Rosenberg's assignment was to discuss the *social* sources of the revival. It is not necessary to parallel his indictment with an enunciation of authentic evidences of prophetic Biblical religion as they have appeared in every community. But with this social background we can recanvass the religious evidences of the revival in America and place them into meaningful context.

In later chapters I shall try to show what this revival has done to our "doctrine of God." America has tended to package God, to make Him more marketable. He has been useful to boxers who fervently prayed as they entered the ring intent on severing their opponents' heads from their bodies. He has ridden—they said so! —with daredevils and racers. He has bided time with and guided the fortunes of motion picture actresses of questionable repute— they said He did. He helped rearrange affairs toward the positive prosperity of men. This last is not wholly new; George Santayana wrote in 1920: " 'Be Christians,' I once heard a president of Yale College cry to his assembled pupils, 'be Christians and you will be successful.' " This was the gospel of America's Gilded Age after the Civil War. But so useful a God is not free enough or strong enough to lift the nation above the secularity which seemed paradoxically to thrive on the latest religious revival. The Gilbert Youth Research Company found that young people during the revival knew little about their religion. Studies of college youth found a religious-minded generation whose values were not shaped by religion in any measurable degree.

In such a season churches were perplexed in their efforts to bring social insight to bear on the ethical situations of the "age of abundance." Sociocritical movements like Christian Action were weakened or even disbanded. The subtraction of God from human social affairs was urged with renewed rigor by many orthodox Christians. Thus in March 1958 the president of the Foundation of the Presbyterian Church in the U.S.A., J. Howard Pew, urged United Presbyterian Men to retreat. He used words that could characterize the whole new antisocial gospel of the religious revival. Corporate involvement in human affairs, he said, violated the Presbyterian principle (John Calvin and John Knox please note!) "Is our Church competent to determine all relationships in social and economic life? Should it become involved in all other secular areas of our common life?" Such involvement, Mr. Pew and others like him feared, might carry with it the prophetic note of social criticism which the churches of the 1930s had used to sting society and their own presuppositions. Such judgment would be incompatible with the safe packaging of God as the Lord of individual lives. Large sectors of the church bought this gospel, at the expense of law. A sermon on this aspect of the revival could take as its text the word of Jesus in Luke 6:26: "Woe to you, when all men speak well of you, for so their fathers did to the false prophets."*

A revised concept of what man is or could be or ought to be became current during and partly because of the revival. This image, we shall see, had little to do with what Protestants in America considered man to be. The new men were manipulated and used. There is a danger that religion under the auspices of a revival such as that of the 1950s could conspire in this manipula-

* Most quotations from Scripture are from the Revised Standard Version of 1946.

tion. The new image often beguiled by reflecting a personal interest of the type which should accompany Biblical religion. It betrayed by proffering a self-defeating "innerism" with narcissistic
appeal. This, according to Emerson W. Harris, was a softening up
of the old-time religion under the guise of old-time religion:

> Faith for what it can do for you is the end result; peace of mind,
> happiness, success are goals earnestly aspired to. . . . Religion, wor-
> ship, God become means not ends. We use them to achieve certain
> goals for ourselves. . . . It is time . . . for the exponents of religious
> outer-ism to become more aggressive, to restore the necessary balance,
> to recover the whole gospel for the whole person.[2]

The churches often found themselves riding the band wagon of
sanctified manipulation of men. They were in position to patternize
men by *ersatz* versions of Christian fellowship in the use of group
dynamics as means toward institutional ends. They could contribute to the passivity of men by preaching the old-time individualist compulsions in a day when individuals could not begin
to carry them out. They could, through borrowed techniques of
persuasion and projection, further confine already closed-in-upon
men. In a time of quest for authentic personhood, the world around
the Church was asking but one question of the spokesmen: not,
Is what they are saying true? but, Are they sincere? Or, to borrow
Hollywood's blurb for the Peter Marshall film, Are they "God's
kind of guys"?

After these discussions of the kind of God and the kind of man
that emerged as a part of the revival of interest in religion, it will
be time to consider the institutionalization of their coming together. A "new religious establishment" seemed to be emerging.
While the revival benefited the churches and profited from the
successes of the churches, a sort of national religion-in-general
knew the greatest gains. The heart of the revival proceeded apart
from the churches, and apart from the classic Christian faith. Thus
Reinhold Niebuhr, writing in *Christianity and Crisis* (January 24,
1955):

> Our religiosity seems to have as little to do with the Christian faith
> as the religiosity of the Athenians. The "unknown god" (referring to
> St. Paul's observation in Athens) in America seems to be faith itself.
> Our politicians are always admonishing the people to have "faith."

Sometimes they seem to imply that faith is itself redemptive. Sometimes this faith implies faith in something. That something is usually an idol, rather than the "God and Father of our Lord Jesus Christ," who both judges and has mercy upon sinful men and nations. Sometimes we are asked to have faith in ourselves, sometimes to have faith in humanity, sometimes to have faith in America.

Niebuhr's judgment applies to the maturing Americanized state Shinto with its analogies in modern Japan and Antonine Rome—a settling new American religion, the agent and the product of the erosive revival of interest.

To be sure, one highly public aspect of the revival seems to be a witness *against* the erosion of distinctions. This is the resurgence of mass revivalism in a form which explicitly identifies itself with the older evangelicalism and draws much of its power from nostalgic appeal to it. This movement for the first time in American history centered in one man. I speak of the wondrous phenomenon called Billy Graham, a towering figure of the decade.

Where does Billy Graham belong in the new shape of American religion? In many respects he represented a massive effort to go against the popular winds. Yet there should be a clue to the answer in his failure to become unpopular with people outside the churches. His appeal to the secular press suggests that "the world" somehow succeeded in taking him captive. As the saying goes, in olden days they stoned the prophets; now they invite them to dinner. Why did Graham draw such enthusiastic approval from those who would prophesy against the sins of America and why was he so popular among the people he prophesied against?

It is true that many dimensions of his work exceeded those of the more limp aspects of the revival of interest. Graham was, incidentally (let this be clear from the outset), a witness against erosive influences. He was first of all a prophet of particularity. Yet Jew, Catholic, "secularist," liberal, and fundamentalist somehow failed to get the point that he was talking about a scandal, the offense of the Cross of Jesus Christ. He softened the offense by what he offered with it. The gulp over the bolus of his avowed irrationalism was ameliorated by the promise of sweetness to follow.

So it can be said that the witness against the packaging of God also packaged Him, confined and contained Him to some extent in the purposes of evangelistic crusades. In his use of techniques of mass manipulation and despite his many well-meant checks the man who aimed to bring men into vital union with God in Christ often contributed to their further depersonalization. The utterer of judgments against the nation somehow tended to be the sanctioner of its *status quo ante*. All this raises the question, What image of America did Graham have in his crusades? And what changes are manifest if we compare him with his predecessors? It is to this question and its corollary that we now turn.

Historians have nominated the evangelist—not the theologian or priest or layman—as the characteristic man of God in this nation. They have placed the evangelist at the center of the rhythmic ebbs and flows of religious interest in the past, and it would be hard to find a chronicler who was not ready to do the same with Dr. Graham in the 1950s. But the men of six earlier evangelical awakenings had suggested continuities in their approach to America. Now a new stream was flowing toward a changed shore, if we can return to the nautical picture. Even the name by which the most recent renewal went suggested *an assumption completely different from the assumptions underlying the past renewals*. Let us consider only one or two past emphases, in conversation with the portrayals of the subject in brilliant books by Perry Miller (*Errand into the Wilderness*), Edwin Scott Gaustad (*The Great Awakening in New England*), and Timothy L. Smith (*Revivalism and Social Reform in Mid-19th Century America*).[3]

In the eighteenth century the Protestant Christian evangelist intended to *awaken* a lethargic total community to find its true self in God. The characteristic response in that time (when Catholic-Jew-Secularist were nowhere near to haunt) was the act of "owning a covenant" which already existed between the community and God. In the nineteenth century he intended to *revive* individual Christians and to ask them to reform the society which was cutting itself off from God. The characteristic response was personal conversion followed by the organization of reforming institutions. But in the twentieth century he *crusaded* against a mass that was somehow estranged and had cut itself off from the will of God, from which individuals must be separated and saved. The characteristic response was personal decision for Christ. By the middle of the twentieth century, a completely different presupposition about the environment of mass evangelism existed in the mind of the evangelist than existed in his public's.

Each revival nudged America nearer to the crusader's position. Perry Miller's book dealt with the original aspect and prospect of America as it was found by the Puritans who first came to complete the Reformation. They were "an organized task force of Christians, executing a flank attack on the corruptions of Christendom." Soon frustrated in their errand they looked to their theology for an out. Their "federal" redaction of Calvinism provided the out, for its theology revolved around the covenant in which a chained God, "one who can be counted upon . . . who can be lived with," served the covenanted community. God's grace could be channeled in a sequence of natural and almost "behavioristic" causes. ("This," said one divine, "is a very comfortable doctrine, if it be well considered.") The covenant became a strategic device for arousing human activity. God had voluntarily engaged Himself to regular, ascertainable procedures.

Some sort of arrangement as this has had to be at the heart of all mass evangelism, and the great Jonathan Edwards knew as much. Perry Miller sees the national significance of this early evangelical revival: "this first occurrence *did actually involve all the interests of the community,* and the definitions that arose out of it were profoundly decisive and meaningful." [Italics mine: store them away for a later reference and point.] The whole community had set the stage for the Awakening. As the cause of religion declined the ministers did something. They told people: "You were baptized in this church, and if you will now come before the body and 'own' the covenant, then your children can in turn be baptized." Owning the covenant became the formalized communal rite. It was—or should have been—the last time in American history that Protestant Christian evangelists could with some plausibility address the community gathered in the church in the spirit of a line from Christopher Fry's play, *A Sleep of Prisoners:* "You were born here [in church], chum. It's the same for all of us."

Professor Gaustad devotes his study to the years of the Great Awakening and its aftermath. He also begins with the idea of the covenant, "which becomes social and political as it was extended to bind a *total society,* saints and sinners, to the active dominion of God." [Italics mine.] It was this revival which provided the cast of American religion that still persists; its durability is another factor in the erosive effect of even Graham's revival.

In the succeeding decades . . . this piety which had inspired so much theology (as with Edwards) found itself thriving on several shades of opinion and eventually on hardly any opinion at all. A pragmatic America and a frenetic frontier asked of the sermon only that it work. If effects were evident in terms of personal reform and multiplying churches, what more was required? Nothing. Thus, the discrediting of "human learning," characteristic of only a minority during the Awakening, later became typical of a majority of Protestantism.

Helping *whole* men in *whole* communities was no longer to characterize American revivalism. Helping *men* in *whole communities* still was, professedly.

Timothy Smith reveals his relish for the revivalism of the nineteenth century. He argues on unashamedly Arminian presuppositions. He quotes Edward Beecher to the effect that the task of American Christians in the nineteenth century was "*not merely* to preach the gospel to every creature, but [also] to reorganize human society in accordance with the law of God." [Italics mine.] In these words the sense of a growing separation between Christian individuals and a lost society was evident. In this changed environment the ferment became pan-Protestant. Pragmatic concerns demanded united effort, at the expense of theological particularity. Arminianism triumphed. "The idea of personal predestination could hardly survive amidst the evangelists' earnest entreaties to 'come to Jesus.' "

Thus did the national faith of the 19th century approach a measure of integration. Lay-centered, tolerant of minor sectarian difference, ethically vital and democratically Arminian, it was a creed of practical piety, and of compassion which went beyond fine intentions.

Redeemed Christians made bridges to this separated community.

Between Smith's terminus and the middle of the twentieth century there was to come more urbanization, and with it a new alienation coupled with the great influx of non-Protestant religious influences. There resulted a total community which was no longer seen to be involved *even potentially* in the covenant. That dramatic evening in May 1957 when Billy Graham faced New York in

Madison Square Garden was the perfect revelation of this fact. As the greatest evangelist of America addressed the greatest city of America for the first time, he charged: "Because we [Americans] are out of the will of God we have lost the will to do right." It is a long path from "you were born here" to "you are out of the will of God." The rootage in Jonathan Edwards was cut off entirely. The form of evangelism in America had come full cycle. It no longer faced a wilderness; its errand was now into Babylon.

Graham confronted a new environment armed with the old technical assumptions of mass evangelism. The rhetoric of sensation was there. Perry Miller quotes a critical Anglican, Timothy Cutler, in what may be the most profound psychological analysis, in the fewest words, of the revivalist's excesses: the speaker told his hearers that "they were *damned! damned! damned!* This charmed them. . . ." Graham had other assets beyond his personal charm and his sense of Biblical authority. He was reproducing an authentic chunk of Americana, a page out of a beloved old family album. This made an appeal out of Protestant strongholds (witness the busloads of crusaders from the Protestant hinterlands) to the religious remnant in alienated urban centers. Evangelists in this era were impelled to seek the cities which were the symbols of the loss of covenanted community and the emblems of total alienation. The blueprint: enter them with the techniques of past "awakenings" and "revivals." But then, with an insight that went beyond rational calculation, a further step: call the efforts "crusades."

Now we are prepared to ask the question toward which this historical summary pointed. How did the crusaded-against react? Eckardt said that when Graham came as David, *Goliath yawned.* But do people yawn when they are told that they are "out of the will of God," that they are *damned, damned, damned?* Timothy Cutler had been right: "This charmed them. . . ." How could this possibly be? How could Graham's denunciations be taken captive and numbed? Because few very seriously read themselves into the pattern of denunciation. American professors of religion-in-general accepted Graham as the most sincere, most eloquent, if somewhat idiosyncratic, preacher of peace with God. They saw themselves as still part of the "total community" whose interests were involved (Miller), that "total society" (Gaustad), that "reorganized human society" (Smith) toward which revivalists were to build bridges in the Arminian period. "You are out of the will of God," then, was taken to mean somebody else.

Who "liked" Billy Graham?

Protestants, Catholics, Jews.

Only the most rigid Fundamentalists found anything to complain about in Graham's theology. Reinhold Niebuhr, *The Christian Century, Christianity and Crisis,* and assorted Episcopalians and Lutherans raised some questions. But few listened. The most fashionably liberal preachers of New York made it clear that except for a few peculiarities of diction and emphasis their message and Graham's was one and the same. In fact it was not the same. Yet he did anything but push them from the platform. Roman Catholics were sufficiently attracted by this Protestant preaching that they had to be warned against doctrinal indifferentism by informed hierarchs. The Jewish hoodlum Mickey Cohen was one of the few particularists. Attracted as he was to Graham, he tried to make clear to a dumfounded press that he could not make the leap because he was a Jew and not a Christian and Christianity had some elements offensive to Judaism.

What I am suggesting is that while Graham was crusading against a lost community, with a specific doctrine of God and view of man in mind, most of his hearers by first and second hand were performing a casual if intricate act of translation. No one was ready to read himself out of the religionized community. All of them accepted Graham's God, allowing him a few eccentricities of expression. No one felt judged.

If it is frustrating to mass evangelists to have this awareness thrust upon them it seems to me that this is simply the way the cards are dealt to them today. Just how they should go about challenging society's presuppositions and arousing some anger is hard to say. Graham gave some indication of ability to raise tempers in his later forays into the South, where his stronger view on non-segregation became an issue. Perhaps mass evangelism can still find ways to make itself really heard. Or perhaps its very nature as *mass* evangelism sets limits upon it.

Thus what had been directed against secularism and religion-in-general, against erosion of theological distinction in the name of evangelicalism, and against prideful religion in the name of repentant Protestantism, experienced great difficulty in being what it set out to be. This is not the place to detail all the assets and liabilities of that phase of the revival which did lie on the border between religion-in-general and the churchly awakening. But as we move on from this central subject several observations are in order.

First, despite its appeal to evangelical orthodoxy it muddied the issue by its extremely "liberal" high-Arminian view of man, preached to men who could not well carry out its individualist ethical injunctions in a highly organized society. Second, despite its professed evangelicalism it fit into the erosive pattern because its spokesman, his eyes on the pragmatic goal of securing decisions for Christ, glossed over theological differences. This approach involved a sleight-of-hand ecumenicity which, while it might criticize the theology of the ecumenical movement, evaded the issues at the heart of that movement's problem and potential.

Third, the nature of the support it solicited in New York and San Francisco revealed the profound appeal of the revival. It was an attempt to deal with urban centers alienated not simply from religion or from Christ but from evangelical Protestantism. It attracted Protestants of diverse viewpoints. Many of them dissociated themselves from one another and the message, but all supported the crusades on the theory that "anything that is happening is better than nothing."

And so in the midst of the Liebmans and Peales and Eisenhowers, the one man who most concerned himself with a Biblical religion of judgment and mercy was not able, despite his best efforts, to provide America with a shelter-belt against eroding winds, a levee against the wearing waters of generalized religion.

It is impossible and by now certainly unnecessary to document fully the nature of the new revival. The story has been told repeatedly from the viewpoint of both supporters and critics. The two points on which all observers seem to agree is that there has been a very broad revival of interest in religion but that it has been accompanied by an increase in secular patterns of thought and ways of living. This brief summary has been necessary to provide the background for our attempt to place the revival in the context of the whole American development, to cite it as an agent of a new, post-Protestant American religion.

In this context it represents the *second* great revolution in American religion. In 1895 the historian of American Presbyterianism, Robert Ellis Thompson, saw the true significance of the Great Awakening of the mid-eighteenth century. That awakening of American evangelicalism, he said, "terminated the Puritan and inaugurated the Pietist or Methodist age of American Church History." It was the hinge from Calvinist to Arminian America. It set the stage for the first half-dozen revivals of religion. *The recent First Great Awakening of interest in religion-in-general is terminating the Pietist age and inaugurating a post-Calvinist, post-Arminian, and post-Protestant age.* The result of the revival has been a heightening of an attitude toward faith and the elevation to ultimacy of a generalized religious interest. This result has dominated at the expense of renewal of distinctive and substantive religious witness. Even the proclaimers of a particular vision have against their will been included in the Protean category of generalized interest.

The cultured despisers of religion, unable to attack the revival since it resided in the bedrock of the mores, could rightfully find the Church vulnerable when it was identified with this bedrock. C. Wright Mills, while he confused what the meaning and message of Christianity are or ought to be with his own invention, did hit the "hot button" in his "Pagan Sermon to the Christian Clergy" in *The Nation:*[4]

If there is one safe prediction about religion in this society, it would seem to be that if tomorrow official spokesmen were to proclaim XYZ-ism, next week 90 percent of religious declaration would be XYZ-ist. At least in their conforming rhetoric, religious spokesmen would reveal that the new doctrine did not violate those of the church. As a social and as a personal force, religion has become a dependent variable. It does not originate; it reacts. It does not denounce; it adapts. It does not set forth new models of conduct and sensibility; it imitates. Its rhetoric is without deep appeal; the worship it organizes is without piety. It has become less a revitalization of the spirit in permanent tension with the world than a respectable distraction from the sourness of life. In a quite direct sense, religion has generally become part of the false consciousness of the world and of the self.

There remains the most disturbing question of all, the one

which the riders on the band wagon of revival have done their best to ignore. D. W. Brogan, a perceptive visitor in our midst, asked the question. After reviewing the signs of revival he predicted that someone, some day, will stop to ask of the religious witness, *Is all this true?* Are the churches ready for the reaction which will be directed not at religion-in-general but at free-wheeling, free-loading riders of the band wagon from among the churches? Before such an hour comes, the churches would do well to shore up their resources of constructive theology. They will have to be ready to take a stand, to speak for truth or to deny that there is such a thing! Faith in faith presupposes no object of witness. Faith in God does. The churches had better be ready to detail their vision of God, their hopes for man, and their picture of community.

There are certain assets on hand against this hour of testing. First, there are the "square pegs" in the round holes of revivalism, the "third force" Protestants who do not fit in, the intransigent groups that are usually spoken of as sects. Part of their appeal arises from the fact that they are talking about something, about certain visions and hopes. They refuse to conform. Also, there are many responsible elements in Protestantism, Judaism, and Catholiscism that have likewise become articulate. What is their role in a time when religion and national life are so fuzzily intermingled? Historian Daniel J. Boorstin has described it:

> In American culture, then, an especially valuable role may be reserved for those religions like Judaism, Catholicism [haven't large parts of these also succumbed?], and the intransigent Protestant sects which remain in a sense "un-American" because they have not yet completely taken on the color of their environment. Such sects, while accepting the moral premises of the community, can still try to judge the community by some standard outside its own history. But even these religions often take on a peculiar American complexion and tend toward validating themselves by their accord with things as they are.[5]

A second asset is the recovery of Biblical theology and the renascence of constructive theology in the several religious traditions and confessions. Symbolic of these recoveries are the names of the Jew Martin Buber, the Roman Catholic Jacques Maritain, the Protestant Paul Tillich. The revival of interest has given these thinkers a certain faddist popularity among intellectuals. It may be that the cutting edge of their ideas has been dulled by this acceptance, much as Billy Graham's appeal was dulled by acceptance in a different sector: but that their probing has attracted a relatively large audience is a hopeful sign that there are those in this country who have a more profoundly critical interest in religion. If surfeit with holiness in general some day brings regurgitating reaction to churches in particular, it will be helpful to be able to point to the fact that the sellout was not complete. Not everyone rode the band wagon.

A third resource is the ecumenical movement. One of the major problems connected with the revival of interest has been its relative isolation. Christianity was meeting hostility in much of the East and indifference in much of the West. In America it was living in a sort of dream world, the type of comforting and comfortable milieu which has smothered the Christian witness in the past. The ecumenical gatherings of the last decade and a half have brought Americans into close contact with men and women who are struggling and dying for the faith, with theologians who must draw their lines with clarity lest they be swallowed up in dissolution or nothingness or absorbed into syncretisms not greatly different from Americanized religion! Americans have often been impatient with the theological probing of these embattled Christians. Perhaps the ecumenical contact will, on this level if on no other, serve as a brake to the band wagon.

The fourth and most inclusive resource of hope is the ongoing endeavor of those who are not seeking "what the Gentiles seek," the people whom one meets in the more prosaic and more enduring life of the Church in local congregations everywhere. This "hidden Church," a little flock which no doubt numbers many millions, has profited from the revival and will certainly outlive it. Nowhere else is the Christian witness more sorely tempted; nowhere else is it more likely to survive.

Two

The God of Religion-in-General

W E COME now to consider the nation's God, the God who is the product of the revival of interest in religion. There is little to say about this God. The most regular and obvious criticism of the revival is that we have been witnessing a revival of faith in faith, a resurgence of an attitude directed toward no particular deity. But even "no particular deity" is a deity, and the worship accorded such a deity is also religion deserving careful attention. Here, then, a brief statement of the doctrine of God as a measure of the nation in the time when it was seeing the triumph of religion-in-general.

It is hard to say who first pointed to the object-less obsession with faith as faith, but William Lee Miller of Yale University pointed to it most accurately. In his statement on "Religion and the American Way of Life" he identifies three problems having to do with religion-in-general:

First, there is the widely prevalent and intellectually debilitating relativism that removes the link between mind or conscience and an objective truth or value. . . . Second, there is the problem of the utter pragmatism of our society. Practical and technical and functional questions are made the primary questions, and the larger ends and meanings of life are either obscured or falsified. We are notoriously inclined to emphasize the short-run, tangible, and quantitative at the expense of the long-run, intangible, and qualitative. [Finally, there is the problem created by] the drive toward a shallow and implicitly compulsory common creed.[1]

31

Relativism. Pragmatism. Compulsory common creed. Facing these, many Protestants have not countered with a new absolutism, a prideful antipragmatism, or a compulsory divisive creed. At their best they have argued that, as it approaches the world, the Church must begin by minding its own business and setting its own house in order. But for the Church to follow this advice inevitably leads it into temptation to succumb to the American "Way of Life" creed. The true test of the Church today is forcefully defined in a statement taken from the journal *Theology Today:*

> Never must the Church sponsor a blanched, eviscerated, spineless statement of confessional theology. . . . It must give birth in this revolutionary transition time to a full-blooded, loyally biblical, unashamedly ecumenical, and strongly vertebrate system of Christian belief.[2]

If this is the task of positive Protestantism today, we might begin by asking, What does it face? The answer is dramatically clear.

No term better describes America's new religious constellation than one we have repeatedly used: "religion-in-general." As a national faith it swirls around the churches and sometimes flourishes in them. And the religious complex which has most to lose in this process is Protestantism, because Protestantism had the greatest investment in the religious situation that has lately been supplanted. When we begin to examine the substance of America's new religion-in-general it becomes clear that it is no nuance but strict historical accuracy to call these post-Protestant times.

The label is not meant to hint at defeatism or despair. As a matter of fact it is vulnerable to the charge that it calls attention to the past. But one could certainly not describe these as post-Catholic, post-Jewish, or post-secular times. They are post-*Protestant;* they are reminiscent of, and draw some of their enduring vitality from, the undeniable Protestant contributions of the past. Nevertheless, a nostalgic Protestantism that chooses to live in the past or to yearn for its return is doomed to frustration. American Protestants are busy these years, whether they always realize it or not, in reassessing their place in American life. For such reassessment neither illusions nor dreams are of help. Rather, we must heed the advice Bishop Gustav Aulén of the Church of Sweden once gave on the question of sacred-secular relations: to begin, "it is necessary to let everything be what it is."

To begin, then, let us recall that this influence of the milieu on religion has been especially noted in America, because the American environment is so congenial to many varieties of religious impulse. Today more than ever this environment is a sort of cosmic Slenderella, polishing the edges and smoothing the roughness of religious particularity. Which is to say that the basic religious concept in any time or place, the "doctrine of God," has also been to some degree shaped by the environment.

It is not doing violence to the facts to say that America has always had a national concept of God and of its own relation to Him. Such concepts as this are extremely durable, protected as they are by their residence in the value systems of masses of people through a number of generations. The original contributions, despite many transformations, help preform many dimensions of culture and religious expression. For convenience' sake, we may speak of the original American expression as being Puritan or loosely Calvinist in nature. It may seem strange to speak of anything as being *loosely* Calvinist, but Perry Miller's comment on the federal redaction of Calvinism (quoted in the last chapter) implies exactly that term. The adjectives, of course, are not to be taken in a theologically precise sense, as "John Calvin's doctrine of God" or "Mr. Puritan's doctrine of God"—neither of which predominated. Rather they refer to a developing theology which was associated with certain Protestant institutions in America.

Perhaps the best and most profound study of the transformations of this Puritan-Calvinist "doctrine of God" that has appeared to date is H. Richard Niebuhr's *The Kingdom of God in America,* a book that wears very well. Niebuhr begins with a reference to one overarching theological viewpoint:

> Any attempt to trace the pattern of the Christian movement in America must begin with the Protestant Reformation. . . . As a religious movement the Reformation was characterized above all by its fresh insistence on the present sovereignty and initiative of God. . . . The fundamental principle of the new faith was the prophetic idea of the kingdom of God.

America, whatever else it was to become, "was also an experiment in constructive Protestantism." A text for this central view of man's relation to God is properly sought in Calvin, as quoted by Niebuhr:

> We are not our own; therefore neither our reason nor our will should predominate in our deliberations and actions. We are not our own; therefore let us not presuppose it as our end to seek what may be expedient for us according to the flesh. We are not our own; therefore let us, as far as possible, forget ourselves and all things that are ours. On the contrary, we are God's; therefore let his wisdom and will preside in all our actions. We are God's; toward him, therefore, as our only legitimate end, let every part of our lives be directed.[3]

If this was the religious idea brought along to America by the Puritans and the various groups which shared the inheritance of the Protestant Reformation, we can only gasp at what has happened to it. Not only is the blighted *result* of the religious attempt obvious today (Calvinism would have allowed for that), but the religious *goal* is outlined in different terms. Nowadays God is often offered in packaged and highly marketable forms. To express it in a perverse rephrasing of Calvin's statement, He is expected to baptize what is "expedient" for man, to concur with man's reason and will. God is ours; we desire that He let our wisdom and will prevail in His actions.

But is there anything new about this at all? Perhaps all through recorded history this planing down and easing off has been the temptation of religious men torn from their theological roots, has appealed to what theologians used to call the "natural man." What is new is the institutional sanction accorded this concept in American religion. God is Himself predestined by national fiat and by popular acceptance. To borrow an overworked current phrase, God is "other-directed." He takes His signals from His peers, the men who fashion Him. What happened between the original intention and contemporary expression will be explored later. At this point let me substantiate these remarks about the contemporary expression.

Why has an ancient tendency been so exaggerated of late? Why do the winds which erode Protestant particularity in its view of God blow more fiercely today? To ask these questions raises the more complex questions of the motives behind the religious renascence itself. Many of the psychosocial explanations of Milton Rosenberg apply here. But he dismissed too lightly a motive that goes a long way toward explaining why America packages and markets its deity; namely, the failure of nerve. D. W. Brogan provides useful neutral perspective on us and our religious life. In his introduction to a new paperback edition of *The American Character* he remarks: " 'There are no atheists in the foxholes' and America is now in a foxhole that she may have to inhabit for a generation. The consequence of this predicament is that refusal to give lip service, at least, to the American religion is a kind of treason and is punished as it was in the America of a century ago."[4] This foxhole situation is part of the cold and occasionally hot war which has shattered our illusions of American superiority and robbed us of security by bringing us up against competing ideologies that we cannot understand.

The relativist, pragmatist, common-creed religion-in-general which offers such a doctrine of God has, of course, a very strong note of Christian reminiscence. Its creed is borrowed from its Christian memory (had it been born in, say, the world of Buddhism it would carry overtones of that faith). For this reason not all of us recognize how much erosion has occurred. Sometimes we are brought up short to face it. As an example of the reminiscence and the contrast, take the creed of a prominent community church (charity forbids identifying it more precisely) and set it alongside the Apostles' Creed:

Community Church	*Apostles' Creed*
I believe in God, the Father, all-loving;	I believe in God the Father Almighty,
Maker of all that is;	Maker of heaven and earth:
And in Jesus Christ,	And in Jesus Christ
loveliest of His many sons, our friend;	His only Son our Lord:
who was born of the Mother, Mary;	Who was conceived by the Holy Ghost, Born of the Virgin Mary:
moved by the Spirit of God; suffered under the systems of men; was crucified, and died for the sake of truth and right.	Suffered under Pontius Pilate, Was crucified, dead, and buried: He descended into hell; The third day he rose again from the dead:
Yet he lives again in the lives made beautiful by His truth, ascending into the hearts of men,	He ascended into heaven,

Community Church	*Apostles' Creed*
and working at the right hand of God, the Father who works all that is good.	And sitteth on the right hand of God the Father Almighty:
	From thence he shall come to judge the quick and the dead.
I believe in the Holy Spirit of truth, beauty, and goodness;	I believe in the Holy Ghost:
the ministering Christian Church;	The holy Catholic Church;
the communion and cooperation of good men with God and with each other;	The Communion of Saints:
the destruction of sin by righteousness;	The Forgiveness of sins:
the worth and beauty of human personality;	The Resurrection of the body:
and the everlastingness of the life that is in God. Amen.	And the Life everlasting. Amen.

The two creeds share "Amen" and many other words, but that is about as far as the similarity goes. In spirit they are totally unlike each other. Indeed, it is with some trepidation that I quote the community church creed, thus making it available to so many other churches in need of a creed! The author is unknown, but it smells strongly of committee work. In any case, it is an eloquent definition of religion-in-general.

Perhaps it would be worth while to look for a moment at this creed as an example of generalized religion's resolutions. Admittedly there is much that is offensive in the Apostles' Creed—it is intended to be. But it would have cleared the air had the writers of the community church creed made an altogether fresh beginning. Here was, indeed, a phrasing of Christian reminiscence. Most people who read or recited this creed would feel at home with it, might even think they are affirming what C. S. Lewis has called the "Same Old Thing." But they are not. They are either avoiding or denying the following:

The almighty power of God;
an expression of a belief in "heaven" in any sense;
the uniqueness of Christ;
His Lordship;
the Incarnation;
the bluntly historical note (Pontius Pilate);
the defeat of Jesus' death;

the descent into hell—whatever was meant by that phrase;
an ascension any "higher" than the hearts of men;
judgment;
the Holy Spirit of God;
the holiness of the Church;
the forgiveness of sins by God;
the resurrection.

Now of course people have a perfect right to devise a religion
which omits any or even all of these. But Americans tend to borrow
Christian coloring for a harmless little divinity who has almost
nothing in common with the God of Christianity.

Precise definition of this little divinity, this God of religion-in-
general, is difficult, not because He is so remote but because He is
so near, cuddled up right next to us. Yet we can discern His general
features.

First, He is understandable and manageable. When men are bewildered in foxholes they want a cozy relationship with a comfortable God. Earthly knowledge has become too high for us; we cannot
attain it. It has become too complex for us; we must contain its
source. "The great properties of knowledge today," scientist J.
Robert Oppenheimer told the International Press Institute, "are
these two: It is mostly new—it has not been digested—and it is not
part of the common knowledge of man. It is the property of specialized communities who . . . by and large, pursue their own
way with growing intensity further and further from the roots in
ordinary human life." With earthly knowledge too high, it is desir-
able to bring heaven down. When God became the property of
specialized theologians, generalized peddlers took Him over and
redesigned Him for mass consumption.

Second, religion-in-general's understandable God is comforting:
this is the obverse of the Christian doctrine of the Incarnation, in
which God both veils and reveals Himself. Allan Nevins, in a historical "Assay of an Epochal Quarter-Century" (*New York Times,*
March 30, 1958) concluded that "terrors and assurances have been
about equally balanced during the twenty-five years [1933–58]."
If God must calm the terrors of men, He must also be on hand to
sanction their assurances.

This was certainly the case in their country in the 1950s. When
America emerged from the shelters of the nineteenth century and

entered the world she found herself in need of exportable ideologies. She had gotten along without them for a couple of centuries, but now the bare cupboard of national ideology had to be filled. The keepers of the cupboard borrowed from religion: godly democracy was the best foil to "godless Communism."

Like the college student of 1958 who, according to the editor of the *Minnesota Daily,* "wants something he can put his hands on; the double meaning is not popular," the nation was no longer content with a mysterious deity. It wanted to establish what William James described with favor as "proper connection with the higher powers." There seems to be nothing wrong with that.

As was pointed out earlier in this book, "godly democracy" became a cold-war slogan. On the national level, the President reminded us that our country was "the mightiest power which God has yet seen fit to put upon His footstool." In the domestic market, as we have suggested, the prophet of the 1950s was Norman Vincent Peale. There is no question but that Peale's sermonizing passed the relativist test: what he said as a Christian minister seemed true to everyone. It passed the pragmatist test: what he said seemed to work. It was adaptable to the pressures which sought to impose a common creed: there was little in it to offend anyone. And Norman Vincent Peale did help many people in the 1950s. In a world where any act of love is superior to an act of hate, where understanding is more to be sought than misunderstanding and restored relationships than broken ones, where hope is rare—in such a world Peale's achievement was not to be discounted. But in our context more serious questions must be asked of his approach as an exclusive strategy. He was speaking out of Protestantism with the gospel of positive thought denuded of Protestant substance. Whenever questioners in his magazine columns pushed him to the wall concerning his attitude toward historic Christian teachings he affirmed them—and then dropped them from discussion. For historic Christian teachings have something particular and exclusive about them: every antagonist of the faith has known this. But the particular and the exclusive are not a tasty dish for mass consumption.

The pithiest condensation of this type of promise or gospel was offered by Charles H. Clark in *Brainstorming.*[5] Clark suggested that men should take pencil and paper to church because "some people get their best ideas in church." He not only saw nothing irreverent about this; he found the highest sanction for it: "The Lord gives us an extra reward for going to church, for in church we are at peace with the world and our subconscious throws out ideas it has been working on." Interestingly, in the alphabetical catalog of Dr. Peale's publisher, "Self-Help" as a category follows "Religion" (Peale himself is listed under "Inspiration"), so that if the God of positive thinking provides us with uncertain guideposts we may still help ourselves on the road of life with "Auto-conditioning," "Subconscious Power," "Creative Power of Mind"—all of which read just about exactly like the positive thinking which has a Protestant orientation.

A third mark of the God of religion-in-general is that He is one of us, an American jolly good fellow. Popular songs—which may be beamed at the masses instead of rising from them, but do reflect the temper of the times—reveal this. In this connection Bible-believing Miss Jane Russell's reference to God as a "livin' Doll" has been most frequently quoted. Then there is the cult of the "Man Upstairs," as analyzed by A. Roy Eckardt: "God is a friendly neighbor who dwells in the apartment just above. . . . Thus is the citizenry guided to divine-human chumminess. . . . Fellowship with the Lord is . . . an extra emotional jag that keeps him [the citizen] happy. The 'gospel' makes him 'feel real good.' "[6] Sometimes, when instinct winces at such blasphemy, God is identified as Someone in the great somewhere, or simply as "He."

This comfortable familiarity, this divine-human chumminess goes a long way to explain what puzzles so many: the coincidence or our nation's greatest revival of religious interest with its most excessive outburst of secular impulse. No one has complained of this more than the most successful revivalizers. Dr. Peale never tires of berating women for wearing low-cut dresses. Dr. Graham is exasperated with almost every aspect of our culture and social mores. Their colleagues all complain that the revival has not gone deep. Indeed, in the years of the revival America was more comfortable and prosperous than ever before. More people spent more money on gambling than ever before. The sex novel and the dirty magazine came into their own. Levels of sacrifice were minimal. But the "revived" and "secularized" communities were not two different sets of people: there was significant and obvious overlapping. Why? Is not the divine-human coziness a "theologization" of Smerdyakov's nihilistic atheism? A nonexistent God and a completely captive God are very much alike; under the one or under the other "all things are permissible."

Something sympathetic should be said concerning the confluence of these three marks of the deity of religion-in-general with Christian doctrines. In Christian theology too God reveals Himself; He does not remain remote. But this is far from becoming understandable and manageable. The Christian knows in part and prophesies in part. God's ways are not man's ways and God's thoughts are past finding out. His condescension in His revelation in Christ does not exhaust the mystery. Second, He comforts. The direction of Christianity is toward the Good News:

> Go and tell . . . what you hear and see:
> the blind receive their sight and the lame walk,
> lepers are cleansed and the deaf hear,
> and the dead are raised up,
> and the poor have good news preached to them.
> [Matthew 11:4–6]

But Christian revelation recognizes a double-sidedness to all of life. It knows the endurance of doubt, despair, and temptation. It calls men to carry a yoke and to bear a cross. It does not promise ready solutions to all the external problems of life. It offers a crown; but "no cross, no crown." Religion-in-general makes no provision for the yoke or the cross. Third—and here the contrast is deepest and sharpest—in place of a jolly good American fellow, the Christian revelation pictures God as sovereign and majestic and holy. When He unveils Himself, "The Lord lays bare his holy arm." To suggest that He is a sort of folksy dodderer sitting in a rocker upstairs is the height of blasphemy. "Someone somewhere" may live upstairs, may be a "livin' Doll," but this is certainly not the Lord of Hosts, the God of Jacob, the Refuge of men.

Religion-in-general is the result of a gradual conjunction of one side of the American creed with one side of the Christian revelation. The one side of each is a rich great blessing when seen in relation to its obverse, but to split the coin is to make problems. Yet this conjunction of the separated sides is the "wave of the future," according to our most sophisticated foretellers. Perhaps the most informed and respected of these, Henry Luce, remarked in 1955 on "the merging of the gospel of work" ("free enterprise") and the "social gospel" ("humanitarianism").[7] Note incidentally the secularizing translation of what is really a technical term that should be used with some precision: social gospel. According to Luce the merger of these two rivers with a third, the river of Science, has made the sea of abundance around which the Western world now lives.

Instead of the horror of Orwell's 1984 we are having the glory of Luce's 1980. Borrowing a concept from Lecomte du Noüy, Luce speaks of a future collaboration with God in charge of evolution as the American pattern. This is a new vision with familiar overtones.

On the one hand, "collaboration with God" would almost perfectly define "the American religion"—the religion so easily condemned as overoptimistic, complacent, and shallow. The American word, before evolution, was Providence. While on the one hand the American was open to Infinity (cf. Emerson and Whitman), on the other hand he busied himself with a concrete and limited task. The common task, besides individual salvation, was the winning of a continent and the making of a nation dedicated to a proposition. Now we must see this task as having been a limited one, perhaps even accomplished. And while judging "the American religion" to be parochial, and lacking in the sense of tragedy, may we not also see it as a primitive, crude prefiguring of the du Noüy vision?

Collaboration with God in the whole of evolution—this is a vision so new that it may even be regarded as dangerous in its sweep. For it is nothing less than at last to Christianize Atlas, to unchain Prometheus on his own recognizance, to create a greater Renaissance which shall not become pagan, and to suffuse Lord Russell's dark, icy cosmology with the light and warmth of Christian love and sacrifice and hope.

"Collaboration with God in the *whole* of evolution"—how did this issue from the Protestant vision of response to a God whose ways were ultimately past finding out? How did "God" move from "Providence" to "evolution" in Luce's accurate summary? In tracing this development we see how far America has wandered from its generative Protestant witness, "the present sovereignty and initiative of God . . . and the prophetic faith of the kingdom of God."

This movement toward a packaging of deity is not to be credited to, or blamed on, the environment alone; nor on the "secularists," whom Christians too often make scapegoats and whipping boys. Protestantism itself, in its transformations and acquiescences, helped bring about the change. The winds of erosion first blew in the original adaptations of Calvinism to the American scene—a process brilliantly chronicled by Perry Miller in his *Errand into the Wilderness*. The federalist or covenantal idiom in Puritanism, which forced God to keep His half of the bargain, was the beginning of the effort to manage Him. He became "a God chained—by His own consent, it is true, but nevertheless a God restricted and circumscribed," a God to be counted on and lived with. Man could "always know where God is and what He intends," says Miller.[8] The obvious successes of the Puritans confirmed this relation; Providence seemed to favor the Protestant endeavor.

The Arminian turn in the road accentuated all of this; Christian men and women in community with a heightened activist impulse attempted and achieved great things for God. There is nothing wrong about such an approach to religion and life and there is very much right with it. But as it merged with the progressivist impulse in the national ethos the specifically Christian orientation tended to vanish. Arminianism keyed the revivals of evangelicalism just as it did the development of Unitarianism's liberal and optimistic theology. In both movements God was necessarily made less mysterious and more manageable.

Extra-Protestant forces were not dependent merely on a quiet impulse in the ethos. They were propelled by the easygoing rationalism of the founding fathers. Yet even their natural religion with its reference to an aloof but holy Supreme Being is far removed from the divine-human chumminess of America in the 1950s. All through the nineteenth century the eroding winds blew. In reviewing that century's revivals Timothy Smith found that orthodox Calvinism, "the bogeyman of social historians," was a dying dogma. Meanwhile revivalistic Calvinism began to take on an Arminian look. This fusion of viewpoints characterized the bulk of American Protestantism. Almost all but high-church Episcopalians, old Lutherans, old school Presbyterians, antimission Baptists, and a smattering of confused Congregationalists shared the relaxed yet creative central position. Roman Catholicism, according to recent historians, also found this optimistic and activistic orientation congenial. The fact that Calvinists, Arminians, and Roman Catholics could so comfortably share one orientation suggests the enduringly Christian character of that emphasis. This makes no brief, however, for the twentieth-century version of that emphasis, now secularized beyond the imaginings of the past.

Yet God has never been left without witness in America. There have always been and there still are those who can bring Good News because they participate in the depths of tragedy and the breadth of judgment. Curiously, correctives to this overemphasis on man's chummy relation to God have often come from unorthodox and even nonreligious sources. Here, as often elsewhere, American Protestants owe much to many who are so easily dismissed as secularists. When Abraham Lincoln, who was certainly not an orthodox Christian, affirmed that "the Almighty has his own purposes" and that finite men are judged and saved by the Infinite Whose will prevails, he spoke in language quite other than that more recently heard from the White House. The tragic sense of life persists in the literary tradition—from Hawthorne, Melville, and James (who, interestingly enough, claim the attention of many constructive theologians today) to O'Neill, Faulkner, Arthur Miller, and Thornton Wilder. Perhaps the realism that got away from the children of light was picked up by the children of darkness come to help them.

The theological revival of the past quarter-century has found it necessary, in order to dissociate itself from the packagers of deity both in and outside Protestantism, to re-explore the Biblical witness, the original Protestant Reformation, the American realist literary tradition, and contemporary Continental thought. The renascence began with Walter Rauschenbusch's revisionism in his later work. Reinhold Niebuhr and Paul Tillich were the first to move against the stream by asserting the distance between the aspirations of the creature and the ways of the Creator. The profundity of their concern and the audience they have received stand in bold relief against the background of a nation whose religious symbols remained Dr. Peale, Dr. Graham, Mr. Eisenhower, or, on a lower level, the producers of the "Man Upstairs" kind of music.

Widespread dissatisfaction with the limitations of religion-in-general is voiced in every thoughtful gathering of laymen. These people express concern over the image of national religion presented by mass media of communication. They take hope from reflective magazine articles of the type that began to appear in secular journals toward the end of the first phase of the mid-century revival. Many of these laymen would join a thoughtful Christian clergy in stating the choices Biblical religion faces in the erosive milieu of religion-in-general. The choices can be phrased most simply in relation to the doctrine of God:

If Protestantism wishes to be absorbed in this post-Protestant movement it must decide whether it believes God can be packaged or not and whether it believes He is subject to man's manipulations or not. At the very least, Protestants must begin by measuring the distance between present positions and the original ones. They must note the extent of erosion. And such reference to what was places upon the heirs of the Reformation alive in a time like this responsibility for reintroducing the prophetic note. At present someone else is calling the signals. Longing for the good old days avails little. Classical Protestantism is in this respect a minority viewpoint, miles from any position where it could inform American religion in its most recent expression.

Can it be expected to take an ancient road in a new day?

> The voice of one crying in the wilderness:
> Prepare the way of the Lord,
> make his paths straight.
>
> [Matthew 3:3]

Three

Man in Religionized America

N<small>O DISCUSSION</small> of religion can go very far before it faces "the doctrine of man." Theology and anthropology are intricately intertwined, and theological change more often than not is a reflection of a changed view of man and his universe. No doubt this is the sequence in America today: the new shape of our national religion is emerging because the position and stance of man are different, and our conceptions of what man is and ought to be seem to be changing. How do the new images of man differ from those that prevailed in the American past, particularly insofar as the religious impulse is concerned?

The moment this subject comes up we face a difficulty presented by the secular social analysis of the 1950s—a difficulty that could be defined as a tyranny of false alternatives! Most of those who study man today are divided into two camps. One group—made up largely of advertisers, politicians, and businessmen—is undisturbed by what is happening. It looks for the comforting dimensions of "conformity." The other group, the critics, tout "nonconformity" and insist on rebellion of some sort or other. Just why the question was ever posed as an antithesis—as though the only choice before man were between conformity and rebellion—would itself be an interesting subject to pursue. However, we must begin with issues as they are stated.

Yet if we accept the conformity-nonconformity formulation of

45

the social analysts we are from the outset tyrannized to some extent. Possibly we shall derive the wrong answers because we have asked the wrong questions. During the past several years all of us— generalizers, historians, journalists, sociologists, and readers—have been engaged in a somewhat comic dance in a hall of mirrors. (I don't know about the physical or optical aspects of this next picture, but it commends itself to use.) The analysts have placed "man" between two sequences of mirrors of the kind seen in fun houses at amusement parks. One set of mirrors elongates the model; the opposing set broadens him and makes him squat. To pursue the parable: one group of analysts elongates man into autonomous if not arrogant individualism; the other levels him down to robot conformism. The two groups have competed, each attempting to be ahead of the other in knowing which way to turn man at a given moment.

The dance began somewhat in this fashion: "Man" was going about minding his own business when someone, somewhere, pushed him between the mirrors. He chose the elongated one and announced that America was the land of rugged individualism, of a crude do-it-yourself instinct. How long he worked with this image is hard to tell. Early in the 1950s, however, a school of sociologists turned "man" around toward the leveling mirror and warned that America was losing its old individualism and men were more and more conforming to one another's patterns. The advice and the cry then became, "Unconform!" Ever since the sequence has been dizzying.

Obviously, if analysis becomes unanimous, no one can start arguments or sell books. So a new breed of sophisticates emerged, turning conformist man to the other mirror and mocking the sociologists. *"Without the latest password we'd never know what's wrong with us,"* says the man in a Jules Feiffer cartoon.[1] And in a *New Yorker* cartoon the wife of the bearded abstractionist artist asks him, *"Why do you have to be a nonconformist like everybody else?"*

This short-lived school of out-sophisticators of the sophisticates was turned from its rediscovered elongating mirror back to the leveling mirror as the charge was made that criticism of anticonformists was becoming stereotyped. Of course, this stance could not long be held either. As of this writing, the newest stance (which will certainly be out of date before this reaches readers' eyes) is represented by Morris Freedman's article in the *American Scholar,* as quoted in *Time,* December 15, 1958. Nonconformism, says Freedman, is getting to be more orthodox than conformism, particularly among intellectuals and in the professions. The self-elected nonconformists are culpable on every count on which they attack conformists: There is no more self-righteously, high-mindedly closed mind than that of a nonconformist:

> If nonconformity is to have its rightful say in American life, as it did with Emerson, Thoreau, Whitman and Veblen, it must stop making a fetish of itself. Conformity . . . may, in the end, prove to have the greater attraction for those genuinely seeking a free and full life. After all, unrestricted amateur nonconformism is one of the honorable paths in American history. In the meanwhile, we must oppose all efforts of the dedicated nonconformists to make us not conform according to their rules.

And then someone turned "man" the other way again, toward the other mirror . . .

This overcomplicated picture illustrates the absurdity of tyrannous false alternatives and the difficulty presented by them. In other words, nothing really new is being added by this competition between schools of analysis. For our purposes, it is most profitable to turn back to the researchers of the early 1950s, who first pointed to the new kind of American man—the Erich Fromms, the David Riesmans, the William Whytes. After these, the rest was imitation or variation on an original theme, and that original theme was in its own way most profound.

These social analysts have been telling us for some time now that the men and women who are shaping American religious response today are startlingly different from their fathers. Bone and flesh of the fathers' bone and flesh they may be, but they have been battered by the winds of a later day and have retained little of their heritage. If there is any truth to this assertion, then the part played by these New Americans in religious change deserves study. For remember, ours is a nation where the culture of the people is thoroughly interwoven with their religion. And indeed it is difficult to find any vestige of that particular view of man's potential which was once representative of the broader experience of an American informed by evangelical Protestantism. The frontiersman, the do-it-yourself religionist, the pioneer—those heroic figures of our national mythos—may still exist, but they are the exceptions. And they operate under social pressures and compulsions that their fathers never knew. Evangelical Christians are themselves hemmed in in ways that religious programs and appeals seldom recognize.

By now we are perhaps wearyingly familiar with the secular description of the changes toward other-direction, the organized life and the crowding world. But it remains to place this analysis into a meaningful context of religious history. For what is happening is in many senses unique to America. A different nation with a different history and a different religious reminiscence would produce a different sort of response. The "Russian soul," for example (as most of us have come to think it was in the days before the terror), was the product of many elements in environment and in idea-world, and not the least of the influences that shaped it was the mystic richness of Orthodox religion. The Japanese character shows the effects of the Shintoist or Buddhist elements that have fused with the broader national experience. And the stereotype of the Scotsman includes some of the rigor of the Calvinist thrust in Scottish history.

The "American spirit" was formed and informed—so far as religion played its part—in the development by Puritan and, later, by evangelical Protestantism. Even today, when the nation tries to assess credit or blame for things as they have turned out, its memory harks back to this religious ethos. Boasting Protestants and complaining Catholics and Jews keep the memory alive, and their intuitions are by no means to be dismissed. From time to time social analysts have found themselves operating with this picture of the religious ethos in mind—some of them explicitly, others implicitly and after "demythologizing" the picture.

One of the explicitists was William Whyte, whose bestseller *The Organization Man* added a new term to common American speech. Whyte stumbled on to a useful theme through an incorrect use of a term, but it is to his credit that his instincts led him to seek in the right place. In his book he asserts that the *Protestant ethic* is being replaced by a *social ethic*. He has been widely criticized for his use of both phrases. "Social ethic" has acquired many connotations that his indictment fails to take account of. But his use of "Protestant ethic" was even more vulnerable; for to most people who know anything about it, this phrase is a sociological description by Max Weber of the Calvinist compulsion to hard work, competitive struggle, individualism, and thrift.

No doubt the latter criticism is especially justified. It seems hardly necessary to take the long road of a Genevan pilgrimage to find the short way home to an American ethic, and it seems futile to re-explore the elements of common genesis shared by capitalism and reformed Christianity. All this said, however, it remains true that Whyte, in groping for a meaningful term, found it, whether by accident or by intuition or by deliberation. Let us retain the term and reinvest it with meanings acquired by the American experience. For at least a century and a half the view of man that prevailed in the United States was one nurtured by a congenial confluence of Protestant preaching and a free and open environment. That "Protestant ethic" is the one that is being displaced today by an ethic broader than Whyte's "social ethic" would imply.

Massive evidence in the literature and social criticism of the decade pointed to the emergence of a new American, the patternized, passive, pressurized product of a mass society. For years we had been told by cosmopolitan philosophers that he would appear. Karl Jaspers, José Ortega y Gasset, Paul Tillich, Karl Mannheim, George Orwell, and others who had stared the storms of the times in the face and read their signs had described the psychic damage these external events would cause on a universal scale. Some of their predictions began to be proved right in the United States during the depression of the 1930s and the war of the 1940s. But it was in the 1950s, with their paradoxical combination of an economy of abundance and poverty of spirit, that their prophecies were largely brought to realization here.

It is true that the conception of a mass society to which these thinkers referred was itself a stereotype open to caricature. Yet who has not felt the effects of this "mass society"? As these men saw it, the world was shrinking. In many respects this shrinkage was a delayed consequence of the industrial revolution that began two centuries ago and more. In particular, technological revolutions in transportation and in the means of communication have diminished the size of the planet. Men are brought into closer contact with one another in most ways, whatever seas of psychic distance and ideological rigor separate them. "We're all in this together." "No man is an island."

Division of labor has made men more interdependent. Meaning in vocation is no longer found in an independent sense, as when a craftsman produced and marketed a product by himself. Now meaning is found only in interrelations and in sequences. When men are so interlocked with one another's destinies, disturbance in any part of society starts a chain reaction that eventually affects the whole. But while external interdependence has increased, individuals more and more experience estrangement and separation from one another. Old ties of family and local community (primary, face-to-face, person-to-person relations) have been torn by mobility and the speed of change. Ancient parochial and provincial faiths are called into question. Few unifying values have taken their place. In exchange for authentic faiths America knows surrogates invented and imposed by manipulators of men.

Meanwhile no accepted critical elite is on hand to influence opinion and taste effectively. The result is a continued flux in mores and morals. Individuals are related to one another secondarily, accidentally, momentarily, tangentially, in compartmentalized fashion, instead of organically. Spatial and social mobility—man on the move from place to place and from status to status—has caused further disturbance. Dress and title no longer designate class, and every person acquires a multitude of roles and has to "make good" in many new situations.

Here is where the threat to the individual is most apparent. The person loses a coherent sense of self. The oversized problems of his day add greatly to his personal anxieties. As a result of frustrations he is involved immediately in a quest for new faiths, at times impassioned and at times halfhearted. He can turn in several directions. In a large part of the world he has turned to the charismatic leader, the secular messiah who bestows on each individual a semblance of necessary grace and a substitute for personality. The leader himself is a prop replacing the unifying beliefs of the older society which the mass society destroyed. We have seen this process clearly in Fascism and Nazism, where men willingly surrendered

all semblance of individuality. "The great thing about our movement," said Hitler, "is that these members are uniform not only in
ideas, but even their facial expression is almost the same." It is no
less clear in Communism, whether in the ant heap commune system
of Red China or the idea-plus-power fanaticism of Russia.

There are other directions to turn, and America has chosen these.
While demagoguery has had its day here, this has not been the
major direction in the United States. President Eisenhower did
assume some of the proportions of the charismatic leader, but he
was unwilling and unable to take on himself the mantle of messiah-
ship and was incapable of articulating a new dogma for America—
for which God be thanked! We shall have to look elsewhere for
Americans' psychic adjustments to mass society. Most of these adjustments are found in the use of resources in an economy of
opulence and consumption. They are colored by response to the
advertisement and the sense of leveling in the middle classes. In
such a time of flux religion has seemed a sensible balancing agent.

All this, of course—the reader was warned—is a stereotypical
description.[2] But, as Daniel Bell points out, the stereotype applies
very aptly to today's kind of society:

> In a world of lonely crowds seeking individual distinction, where
> values are constantly translated into economic calculabilities, where in
> extreme situations shame and conscience can no longer restrain the
> most dreadful excesses of terror, the theory of the mass society seems
> a forceful, realistic description of contemporary society, an accurate
> reflection of the *quality* and *feeling* of modern life.

However, says Bell, as soon as one attempts to apply the theory
of mass society analytically it becomes slippery. Like the shadows
in Plato's cave, the stereotypes produce only silhouettes. Each of
the statements making up the description may be true, but not all
flow from one another so simply. Nor are all the characteristics
necessarily present in any one time or place. No organizing principle holds the elements in a coherent, historical, and logical whole.
In other words, generalizations are always full of gaps and "ideal
type" pictures are always limited.

With these cautions in view we shall nevertheless draw an over-
all picture of the American version of man in mass society as
secular social analysis sees him. Here the picture will be constantly

silhouetted against a religious version. Let us hope that, in the cameraman's term, some stereorealism appears from this multi-dimensional portrayal.

It was when Americans awoke to their involvements in the universal stirrings that the new major prophets appeared. Few of their hearers panicked, and few resented the criticisms. Instead of stoning the prophets, Americans elevated them to bestseller ranks. The man in the broadening mirror turned out to be Mr. Narcissus. The people who were being described in the new anthropology were not aborigines, Dieri, or Maori tribesmen, and the rites of their social dance were not primitive initiation ceremonies. These were living, breathing Americans. These were we. The analysis was recognized as being gently on target.

Several features of the analysis are especially notable. In addition to its paradoxical popularity (who believed these critics when they complained that Americans did not enjoy criticism?), its consistency stands out. Our hall-of-mirrors picture was designed to suggest that an antithetical reading of *homo Americanus* was put forward to counter the original analysis. But since the nonconformists were suggesting nonconformity from something, and the unconformists were implying something else to "unconform to," their sophistication was but the other side of the same coin. Another remarkable feature is the contemporaneity of this social history; it did not await the end of an age to be written. The very techniques that had helped produce the new kind of man—I.B.M. and other electronic machines, poll-taking, rapid communications—helped analyze him. We needed interim reports and we received them in regard to all age groups, vocations, places of residence, and forms of leisure.

The very extensiveness of the literature on the new American—a list of books and magazine articles on the subject would run to pages—is also significant. It bespeaks an interest amounting to obsession on the part of writers and readers alike. And this is a clue to a paradox: *that interest in the human person is so intense in the midst of a depersonalizing age.* Similarly, the ambivalent attitude of the better critics toward the shift in values suggests that nostalgia for the older image of man is no longer creative: We shall have to learn to live with this new American man.

So all is not lost. The mass society has not triumphed completely. The Jesuit scholar Walter Ong has celebrated the persistence of personhood against new odds in state and society.

What happens in the state happens in a parallel fashion in secular life generally, as the smaller, personalized units of activity are absorbed —never entirely, but to a great extent—in the larger, more systematized units which mark our age. As organization moves in, the personal to some extent suffers. For, as Buber again has pointed out, the "I" and the "thou" cannot be organized; only the "it" can be.

And yet, since it is persons who in the last analysis effect organization, it is not surprising that under these conditions men immediately devise compensations for the depersonalizing momentum which organization can develop, and devise the compensations *within* organization itself. At one level, and a low one, there is the "personal touch," the gift which is made by a machine and then "personalized" by having something added to it which had been made by another machine, but which somehow allows one's good intentions to show. At a slightly higher level, there is the personnel director, the personnel consultant, and the counselors who haunt the peripheries of our lives. At a still higher level, men in our day have worked out a personalist philosophy, a philosophy of the "I" and the "thou," thereby making the age which in one way has depersonalized itself into the age more conscious of the human person than any age before. I do not mean that everywhere today the human person is honored more than before: but in the over-all pattern of human society, I believe the person is.[3]

If a person must stand in the hall of mirrors he might at least once in a while look into one like this!

Acceptance (with some reservations) of the portrait of man closed-in-upon in mass society need not imply acceptance of the corollary caricatures or simple identification with its distortions or misuses. There is no need for each person to awaken every day and look for new signals of new compulsions; to ask, Am I, now, a member of the silent generation? the careful? the beat? the conforming? the angry? For a time many sermons, in order to breathe the *Zeitgeist,* took their text from David Riesman; the *miles Christi,* setting out for encounter with the suburban parish, adopted *The Organization Man* as a manual of arms. Religious magazines edited for the student generation included some denunciation or other of conformity in almost every issue. Perhaps the most conformist group in America was the popular and predictable group of critics of conformity.

The call to assertive nonconformity and simple rebellion is of course sterile. The laureates of mediocrity in their San Francisco havens, howling the lostness of the "beat generation," have little more to offer their contemporaries than did the late bohemians of the Village. To counsel rebellion and nonconformity raises persistingly the question of John Cogley in *The Commonweal:* "Unconform to what?' Cultic rebellion usually implies—in mass society it *must* imply—simply an adaptation to a different external norm.

That is why "Rebel!" has not become the central message of the more profound analysts, those who would escape the tyranny of false alternatives. Most of them know better than to measure man simply by the cut of his toga, the slip of his sandal, the flannel of his suit; by the externals of barbecue grill, television antenna, station wagon, or rickshaw. But somehow implicit in the criticism of almost all of them (Will Herberg and Paul Tillich are the kind of exceptions that come to mind) is a nostalgia for the autonomous individualism of nineteenth-century mythology. Whether we mean by this autonomous in the casual sense: man free to be a law unto himself, or in the more precise sense: man obedient to the law of reason apart from theological reference—autonomous man is deeply involved in Whyte's "Protestant ethic" or in Riesman's "inner-directed man" or in the individualist of "good old days" reminiscence. Pushed into the deepest corner and asked what kind of being man *ought* to be, most critics on their own presuppositions would have had to give answers based on the history of the past two centuries of philosophical and religious experience.

It is precisely at this point that church historians part company with social analysis in its secular orientation. While evangelical Protestantism helped provide the soil for such an autonomous man, its planting intended a very different growth. The man who belongs to the nineteenth-century mythology was shaped by a religious viewpoint about his origin, his place under the sun among his fellows, and his destiny. The proclaimers of the Gospel in that season spoke of this viewpoint as being "Arminian" (as opposed to "Calvinist" within Protestantism, and as apposed to "non-Protestant" and "nonreligious" in general). Let us hold up the Arminian stereotype of man, what he was and did, and then compare it with the post-Arminian man of today.

Arminianism as a doctrine of man when used by American

frontiersmen and revivalists (yes, they used the formidable term, in heated debate and in quiet discourse!) here referred not to the specific teachings of Jakob Arminius, the sixteenth-century theologian. Instead, picture a native and somewhat naïve American growth: the robust, inventive, and activistic man produced by American evangelicalism, the man who was under compulsion to work out his own salvation in fear and trembling, knowing that "God [was] at work in him, both to will and to work for his good pleasure." This Pauline and Protestant paradox was alive in all the Reformers and was compatible even with the strict Calvinism that Perry Miller described. In this kind of Calvinism "there were possible explanations of how, in spite of absolute decrees, men were required to do their utmost, as though all depended upon them and not on foreordination. In the looser forms of Calvinism there was less difficulty in asserting at one and the same time that God determines but man must perform." As the looser Calvinism was transformed into Arminianism in America more and more was laid upon man. His obvious successes in the New World seemed to certify God's stamp of approval on the doctrine. Activism was normative in religious and vocational lay life.

This activism may have been individualism, but it was *individualism with a vertical dimension,* lived out under God in a way that "Enlightened" individualism was not. If this was individualism, it was not selfish in the way that much rationalist "inner-direction" had been: it was personhood developed in community. This community aspect of personhood seems to escape most of the yearners for the good old days. The fact is that hyperindividualism belongs to the realm of fancy and mythos. Take the characteristic personages of the times: the frontiersmen, the pioneers, the homesteaders. What was the pattern of their western movement? Instead of being cantankerously inventive isolationists, they *gathered:* at every crossroads there was a little white Methodist meetinghouse and, in competition, a saloon. The spelling bee and the threshing day and the barn-raising and the county fair all are as much a part of the mythos and the remembered heritage as the "individualist" pioneer, but they are too seldom seen as belonging to the full picture of the man of the past.

America, and not Max Weber's Geneva, was the scene in which

the Protestant ethic that is being displaced today was developed. The activists were Arminians, *finding their individuality in community.* They were not arrogant sons of the French Revolution. They provided the anthropological background of the old shape of American religion.

This anthropology developed as a correlative to a theology that was distinctively Protestant but became Americanized. In such an environment opposing religious motifs found it necessary to adopt many of its features. As one example, Roman Catholicism, despite the Pelagian tendencies that sent it veering toward Protestant Arminianism in this respect, time and again had to shore up its defenses against the evangelical image of man. The great struggles of nineteenth-century Catholicism in America can be seen from this vantage. The question of lay trusteeism was phrased in disturbingly Protestant terms and was quelled as a heresy would be. Americanism as a heretical designation, and activism as an epithet, belong to this era of the Roman index of prohibited inclinations. And yet the viewpoint made its way and found many indices of congeniality in the American catalogue.

In his effort to persuade Catholic intellectuals to explore the ties between Catholicism and American life Walter Ong has urged them to study the nineteenth century. In place of the continued attempt to prove a common rootage for the American Constitution and the political theorizing of Bellarmine and Suárez—an attempt to base an endorsement of the Church in America upon the reduction of an issue to European components—he would like to see a study of the later American experience:

> The American intellectual would be much more intrigued by learning what the Church in America has to do with the American experience: with the experience of the frontier, the spirit of enterprise and exploration, the process of expansion; and especially today with the forces at work in a mass, industrialized culture, and with the maintaining and interior development of personality in such a culture. . . . There are obvious connections between the dynamic aspects of American life and the theology of mission and of the Incarnation lying at the center of Catholic teaching.[4]

Even more, there is place for the activism and optimism associated with Arminian man: "With roots not only in social and economic conditions, but perhaps still more in the euphoria of the American evangelical Protestant and his exhilarating 'conviction' of personal salvation, American optimism has real, if equivocal, connections with the Gospel, the 'Good News,' " and this evangelical optimism, despite its disguise of the tragic (as in *Death of a Salesman*), somehow persists and can be oil for the bearings in a mass culture. If Ong is right, twentieth-century Catholicism, to find itself, will have to learn to deal with nineteenth-century Protestantism. It will have to explore its own career in the "predominantly anti-Catholic, although, in the large, curiously benign, Protestant culture of the United States in which it was making its home," and relate itself to the ideas behind the American experience.

Other Protestants of non-Arminian stance cheerfully adopted this as the only alternative. Lutheran theology is purportedly anti-Arminian, but its activist dimensions, its success standards, and its whole American spirit derive from the broader evangelical impulse. By the middle of the nineteenth century many Protestant historians were classifying Lutherans among the Arminians—because they were not Calvinist. This was indeed the Methodist-Pietist era in the broadest senses of those terms. The do-it-yourself religion of revivalism was sweeping the land, gathering men into community and helping them find individuality there by religious reference in response to God's activity in Jesus Christ.

In that layman's century freedom was seen in relation to a relatively free and uncircumscribed God. (We're now about half way down the escalator from the Puritans to Peale.) This was the persisting image of man so well described by Protestant Roger Shinn during a Protestant-Catholic-Jewish discussion in Chicago in 1957:

> Christian freedom is neither the lonely rebellion of an atheistic existentialist nor the self-will of the rugged individualist. *It is freedom-in-community.* [Emphasis mine.] In prayer it addresses "the God whose service is perfect freedom." . . . This image of man . . . differs from David Riesman's image of the autonomous man, who maturely chooses his goals; for though it recognizes choice, it starts from Christ's words: "You did not choose me, but I chose you."[5]

In this relation, Shinn argued, there was a "mystery of selfhood" that could point beyond frustration and despair to authentic tragedy; beyond schemes of manipulation to the gift of salvation from a living God. But when that living God is packaged and marketed, confined and predetermined as he is in our revival of religious interest, then he is no longer himself free to give man true freedom. This is the high price our post-Arminian man must pay for his brave beat world.

Freedom-in-community—this is the point of escape from the tyranny of false alternatives.

Conformity suggests a form of slavery-in-community; but slavery is always undesirable.

Nonconformity suggests a form of freedom-in-isolation; but isolation is no longer possible.

Freedom, then, is the goal for authentic personhood.

Community is the place where we shall have to seek it. All this is a way of saying that this book would be a fraud if it represented another effort at how-to-do prescriptions or if it celebrated an achievement. Rather, it describes a task and modestly points to a direction where the men of today can pick up that task, to "work out their own salvation with fear and trembling; for God is at work in them, both to will and to work for His good pleasure."

Only in the light of this Christian reference to freedom-in-community does the discussion of postactivist man make any sense. For in many respects this is the time of heightened activism; of the do-it-yourself, of the treadmill, the grind, the ulcer, the rat race, and the executive ladder. This is the time of painting according to numbers and sculpting according to colors and cutting according to patterns—just so we are *doing* something. That is activism, is it not? Yet the postactivist, post-Arminian category is apt, for it suggests the frustration that results when activist compulsions are laid upon people who cannot carry them out. The inevitable outcome is frustration, meaninglessness, or apathy. And in the more profound areas of existence—including the vocational and the religious—such compulsions are pressed. Later on we shall consider some ways in which the churches themselves may be contributing to this complication—and also a few ways in which they may be of some help. But this is the proper place to look at the New American against the historical and theological background just presented: to show how far we have come, if we can give any credence to the social analysts of our own time.

In place of the religiously oriented person produced by Arminian and activist Protestantism we have the secularized product which has been described as patternized, passive, or pressurized. The rubric for this summary takes root from a perceptive sentence by Will Herberg: The problem of man today is one of a quest "for personal authenticity in the midst of all-engulfing mass heteronomy." I should like to amplify this in two directions in a "trinitarian" reference. First, a little chart may be helpful:

When God is seen as	Then man is seen as	& the problem is one of	then, today, man is often	in his focus on
Creator	Created	Personal authenticity	Depersonalized	Himself (Patternized)
Redeemer	Redeemed	Theological direction	Illusorily Redeemed	God (Passive)
Sanctifier	Sanctified	Ethical orientation	Invertedly moralistic	Others (Pressurized)

Translated into prose:

If God is the Creator and man is the creature of God, then the problem of personal authenticity arises as a result of depersonalizing pressures which patternize selves. Further, now: if God is Redeemer and man is potentially redeemed, then passive man is in quest of theological direction. Prosperous America is often guilty, in its religious revival too, of offering only illusory redemption in the American Way of Life. And if God is Sanctifier and man is in some sense or other capable of being made holy, then the inverted moralism of the new social ethic is a reflection of how under pressure men build up false ethical responses.

Take them in order: man is depersonalized by his position in the mass, by manipulative devices and advertising techniques, by organizational procedures and marketing programs which make of him an object, a thing. The result is a rubber-stamp culture, a pseudo-togetherness that has been much derided, an attempt to make man more manageable as he belongs and conforms. All this is patently different from the free man in Christian community even if that free man was a product of mass revivalism in the nineteenth century. The creativity of the human person is objectified to serve the organization or to ensure the sale of a product.

Perhaps we have decried overmuch this impulse. It is, after all, an inevitable concomitant of a mass-production society. The advertising man's assignment is to sell as many as possible of a manufactured and homogenized item. In a sense he must say, "Be different from anyone else and drive the new ——— (if he wants to stress individuality at all), and then he must hope that a great number of people will want to be different in this manner. Soon— if he is successful—they are all alike. This approach, as I said, is almost inevitable in the advertising world. The danger comes in when by some osmotic intuition, it is absorbed and becomes a part of a nation's broader personal response to life.

Similarly, the activist pattern of "working out salvation in fear and trembling" which was to infiltrate all of life is supplanted in post-Protestant America by a life best described with fearlessly limp and untremblingly passive verbs and adjectives. Here is a catalog taken from titles in a bibliography on modern man: he is crowded, adjusted, conformed, persuaded, organized, surfeited, tranquilized, homogenized, contented, robotized, manipulated, alienated, engineered; he is careful, conservative, silent, moderate. In this relatively comatose state man can be offered surface redemption, particularly when mass production is coupled with material prosperity.

The Christian churches, which are to save men *from* something *for* something (a tremblingly minimal statement itself!), become embarrassed in their quest for a message. Courage is not necessary. The poet John Berryman has pointed out that in the new situation man can live his entire life in America without finding out whether or not he is a coward. Religious commitment is similarly streamlined. The Protestant Council of New York, according to William Whyte, sent out a directive to speakers on its radio and television programs: "In a very real sense we are 'selling' religion, the good news of the Gospel. Therefore admonitions and training of Christians on crossbearing, forsaking all else, sacrifices, and service usually cause the average listener to turn the dial." The present management of the council has notified me that this rubric is no longer in use. We may take this as another mark of recovery from a nadir—particularly if (and its letter to me said nothing to the contrary) no poll was taken to see whether the original directive was correct or not about the dial-turning.

But if passives best describe man, if even religious response is tailored to minimal commitment, what is left? Postactivist man must "do" something. Like modern aircraft which by means of a supercharger automatically build up from within a new and constant air pressure, so a pressurized man· must re-create constants of his own. Unless he does so he is a "rebel without a cause" or a conformist without a norm. Some have found constants through recovery of Christian theology or a personalist philosophy; others, through an inverted moralistic response. Here is the point at which personal sincerity became the test of qualities of faith. Here the pulpit frequently capitulated. Bishop Bo Giertz of Sweden, on a visit to the United States in 1957, remarked on the moralism offered in many pulpits in place of the Christian Good News. When his remark was picked up in the newspapers the indignant response from many was, What are we supposed to preach—immorality? But our moralism, name-in-print charity, is getting us nowhere. The "decent, godless" people have returned to God with no loss of decency. The showily moral path is part of the organizational climb. Yet, paradoxically, respectable "white collar crime" is at an all-time high, and not long ago the United States Attorney-General was quoted as follows in a national magazine: "Easy tolerance of the so-called white collar crimes has increased in the last decade. . . . The foremost need is to revitalize our standards of ethics and morality." In the Jacobs' study, the "gloriously contented" college students questioned admitted freely that 40 per cent of them cheat in examinations without apology or a sense of wrong-doing; 68 per cent favor punitive action against cheaters who are not friends; only 16 per cent favor it against personal friends.

All these little pictures add up to the stereotype of depersonalized, illusorily redeemed, invertedly moralistic man. And out of them emerges the image of interchangeable men. In all this what is most striking is not the similarity of the externals of this life (rows of houses, tail-fins on cars, et cetera) but the similarity of its idea patterns. William Lee Miller has lauded critics who refrain from discussion of the externals of the new life and has praised one critic who "attacks the *ethic,* the *ideology,* that has accompanied these conditions." Miller thinks it important to avoid the "sweeping sociological dismay that marks some of the literature in this field [in order that man may] fight back within the area in which human freedom is real and human institutions are malleable." Men become interchangeable "not because of overt pressures but because of an inner attitude."[6] I should like to hope that in this brief summary it is the inner attitude and not the external pressure, the capitulation and not the sociological change that have come under scrutiny.

For what is involved in the change of inner attitude is what should concern a religious reporter; and this attitude in post-Protestant America has resulted in a surrogate for religion. The late David Roberts was to the best of my knowledge among the first to see this. In discussing the "corporation's hold on the human person" he placed it in the wider pattern of a "creeping, totalitarian religion." Roberts called it a religion because it "dictates how a person shall find security, self-esteem, standards of value and reasons for living"; and he called it totalitarian because, while the pattern allows for some mobility, under it man "has lost the basic freedom of departing from the pattern itself." All our talk about individualism and free enterprise and democracy merely proves how inextricably most of us are caught in the pattern. Because "we don't dare to look at how standardized, collectivized, and conformist we are" we have to find a scapegoat: a scapegoat will spare us from "having to face ourselves." Yet this substitute religion, Roberts concluded—and he stressed that it is *"the* most potent factor in the lives of many Americans"—is "not only irreconcilable with Christianity, it is not even a worthy form of humanism."[7]

The bluntness points to a dramatic truth: here is a conflict of religions. But it would be singularly un-Protestant to make mass society or the organized life a scapegoat and to fail to see Christian involvement. The churches are often seen as part of the pattern. If they are, it cannot be said that they have been coerced. They capitulated and they surrendered to the degree that they accepted alien norms as their own. To show this aspect of religion's involvement in producing the new kind of American we have summarized the myriad depictions of mid-century *homo Americanus* in a category borrowed from religious history: post-Arminian. For "Arminian-ism" thus can remain a point of departure and a norm for measure-ment; it can serve for reminiscence and conscience and perhaps for direction.

The churchly involvement comes in at every point in this analysis—the packaging of God, the patternizing of man, the capitulation to national religion, the loss of true community—as well as at every point of hope. Let us now take a cursory view of ways in which churches themselves are guilty of contributing to the depersonalization of man, offering illusory redemption, en-gaging in directionless or self-directed moralism.

With few exceptions, if we borrow the findings of social analysts as they take the churches into account, the churches are seen simply as part of the larger picture. Seldom do they appear as centers of creativity, authentic redemption, vital ethical direction. From inside the churches our observations would be somewhat different; each of us is familiar with the exception. But in the face of so nearly unanimous external observation, the least we can do is to say "Thank you!" and to sit down with the evidences and determine our place in the scheme of things.

The traditional charges:

Interdenominational and denominational bureaucracies are seen as paralleling secular organizations in their patterns of compul-sions and motivations. An acquaintance of mine wrote a review of *The Organization Man* and in it asked whether many of that book's analyses were not translatable to the "Denominational Man" who heads the organized side of church life. With alacrity a swarm of officials of his own denomination responded with dissenting letters. The reviewer had not spoken in specifics; evi-dently the shoe fit. The incident is typical. We shall enlarge on it in a later discussion of pressures placed upon the Christian parish.

It demands no great perception to note parallels with the secular practice in the churches' use of mass media to induce and intro-duce mediocrity in patterned response. "In a very real sense we are 'selling' religion." Mass evangelism, for all the worthiness of its goals, indulges in frequent attempts to manipulate persons. The mood of the moment is to conjure up an emotion that should be forged in the quiet of a man's being. It is often accompanied by misleading advertising and exaggerated claims motivated by simple success criteria. The statistical obsession that has captured congregations and church boards contributes to a view of life which depersonalizes people. Life in the green pastures of church growth reveals the extent of religious conformity to secular ideals, patterns, and mores. All this is alleged with almost monotonous frequency from outside the churches.

But it cannot be dismissed as carping and waggery by cultured despisers of religion. Many of the social analysts have turned to religion with some hope; others are curiously ambivalent or ambiguous in their discussion of it. Meanwhile, within the churches, not all the critical fires have been allowed to die. Creative theology has kept the prophetic voice alive, and many have listened. The obvious choices among theologians, for example—Reinhold Niebuhr and Paul Tillich—have scored the uncritical cultural adaptationism of the churches with bell-like regularity and in tones approaching stridence. Tillich has warned that if religion passes in America it will not be killed but will die of a surfeit of its own suburban excesses and successes. Conformity meets criticism in many a sermon of Tillich's. He has compared the situation in the churches of today to the past: "The conformism which threatened Jesus most effectively was the religious conformism of his time." Niebuhr's strictures against churchly acceptance of religiosity are too familiar to need repetition. They have been heard, and they have stung us all.

In the churchly journals the score and the scoring are similiar. Gibson Winter's critique of the churches' suburban captivity in *The Christian Century* was, if anything, more stinging than Stanley Rowland, Jr.'s, critique of the same in *The Nation*. Both writers criticized the churches for contributing to the patternized life of prosperous groupness. Many Protestant criticisms of techniques employed in the Billy Graham crusade of 1957 looked like William McLoughlin's preview review in *The Nation,* which had no religious stake in the outcome. Joseph Sittler has attacked the devitalized gospel of acceptance preached in the newer pulpits: "The cult of acceptance is polite. Polite as hell. It has its own grace; the graciousness of no expectation, the suavity of emptiness, the courtesy of non-significance."

The swank Fundamentalist magazine *His* reprinted Paul D. Clasper's "The Denominational Missionary and the Organization Man," which traces the parallels between pressures to which each adjusts most effectively. As a consequence of this adjustment Clasper sees the growth of a "tragic mediocrity" in missionary work. "The missionary must never forget, even in a day in which adjustment is the watchword, that he must maintain the capacity to be against the Organization as well as for it."[8] W. Norman Pittenger draws the same kind of parallels in church life in general, stressing the dangers to theological freedom in a time of organizational conformism:

A religious body which denies legitimate freedom is in danger of becoming a demonic institution which blasphemously claims to be an absolute; and for such an institution, however long it may appear to be "successful," the judgment is sure. It will be swept "as rubbish to the void."[9]

Student magazines like *Motive,* though they sometimes lapse into faddish criticisms of conformity, have set a pace. The Episcopalian *Living Church* in February 1958 carried on a lively "attack on a sacred cow," namely, the use of "group dynamics" as a gimmick which can lead to mediocrity, the stifling of individual creativity, the removal of redemption from the "redemptive fellowship." The Religious Education Association's concentration on "Sacred Images of Man" in its December 1957 convention in Chicago typified the enlightening new concerns. Research continues apace, offering hope through studies of the Biblical view of man, of the concept and reality of authentic community in Old and New Testaments, and of the Christian witness in most of the centuries when man was not seen to be "autonomous."

Merely to understand the historical situation of man today and of the Protestant ethic in process of displacement is to have some idea of what should be done. The churches force frustrations upon the New Americans when they preach individualistic and autonomous activism in little pulpit moralisms: men cannot carry them out in the new society. As Karl Barth points out in *Christ and Adam,* the Church should not be identified either with individualism or with collectivism: "It understands the true man in neither of these ways."[10] It cannot therefore simply berate conformity and overlook the persons beyond the stereotypes, the men beyond the images.

And we can save our energies by knowing where to look to begin picking up the pieces of a new image of man—in the direction of freedom-in-community, of individuality in the shared life. There are prototypes for this in the Old and New Testaments, in much of Christian history, and in the Protestant American past.

Martin Luther somewhere said that every man must believe for himself just as he must die for himself; we might add, so must every man conform for himself. The possibilities for the Christian are nearly infinite if he is "transformed" in that relation to God in Christ out of which "activism" emerged when evangelicalism was helping to shape America. But the Christian possibilities are not necessarily those that are offered on the surface of "religionized America." There are two complications: a competitive religious situation and a complex milieu. A first step toward helping the New American is to realize that the situation has changed; that vital Protestantism in its view of man will be preaching against the vogue, moving against the stream in an environment it had long found congenial.

Four

America's Real Religion: An Attitude

FREQUENTLY IN the preceding chapters we have spoken of post-Protestant times in America—the implication of the phrase being that the religious aspect of our culture, once informed by Protestantism, now knows a different shaping influence. The competitor for attention in America today is not chiefly Roman Catholicism nor Judaism nor even secularism. Rather, it is an attitude toward religion. Elevated to ultimacy, this attitude has become a religion itself. Indeed, if all its aspects are taken into account it is no doubt already *the* prevalent religion. If evangelical Christianity is to make its witness heard in the new shape of American religion, it must first of all extricate itself from this generalized national religion, must clearly show forth the difference between itself and its competitor. Then it can begin to make its way.

It is ironic that a national religion should have developed in a nation which had not intended to have one. The First Amendment of the United States Constitution reads: "Congress shall make no law respecting an establishment of religion." This has set the legal tone for relations of church and state, religion and nation. Congress has abided by the law. But the people, who refused to vest Congress with legislative power in this realm, have gone about establishing religion in a way more pervasive and more durable than legal fiat could ever have compassed. They have embedded it, or an attitude toward it, in the mores, where it is secure.

The attitude which has been raised to religious ultimacy is the

67

advocacy of support of official religion, an overarching nationalization of that religion-in-general which is the product of the erosion of particularity and which makes religious distinctions irrelevant. Of course, not all the people are participating in this religion all the time. Many of us when made conscious of what is happening work to resist it. This consciousness must be built up before the new climate further blurs what valid lines remain in the matter of separation of church and state and before the ground is prepared for new intrusions by aggressive religious forces.

The temptation to elevate an attitude toward religion to religious ultimacy has been inherent in American life ever since we began to be tantalized by the success of our "great experiment" of religious freedom and the mutual toleration of disagreeing religious groups—as a matter of fact, even before the experiment was successful. It is easy now to criticize the enlightened philosophy of the fathers of the United States, as it is easy to criticize any obsolete pattern of thought. Yet the easygoing latitudinarianism of the Franklins and Washingtons, the Jeffersons and even the Madisons, was a happier solution in its day than were any alternatives then open.

America knew a nascent pluralism from the time two men of different faiths set foot on its shore with intention to remain. At first, by colonies, there was relative homogeneity of official profession, though not nearly so much as the common picture from our distance would allow. Colony after colony saw the official establishment of religion. Congregational-Presbyterianism prevailed in New England, Anglicanism in the Southern colonies. Some of the middle colonies professed and practiced religious toleration or complete religious freedom, but these were the exception.

When the colonies merged their fortunes the question of establishment remained to plague the men of good will who wanted to make one nation out of many elements. The attitude of man to his Maker being a fundamental of the common life, it seemed necessary in a free nation to encourage the free practice of religion. At the same time, few of the shapers of the nation's destiny were willing to see the nation take form in any antireligious fashion. Tacitly, implicitly, unofficially the Federal Government undertook to encourage religion, a step that was accelerated as the individual states dropped their official establishments (by 1834).

From the first there were those who urged the development of a common faith, a formal ideology to present to the world and to nurture the common life. Fortunately, this was resisted. However, a common attitude toward religion was prevalent among the founders, and it was this that later was elevated. Most of the authors of the documents of our freedoms were professing Christians, affiliated with Protestant denominations. Most of them were also influenced by the gentle lights of rationalism, the late eighteenth-century currents of ideas. At the heart of those ideas was the essence of a natural religion: an affirmation of certain basic beliefs in God, in justice, in retribution. It was implied (though Franklin and Jefferson in particular *articulated* this) that what the individual sects held particularly beyond their equipment to inculcate morality was irrelevant and perhaps divisive.

Promulgation of this attitude toward particularity has never been assigned to any governmental official. The American religion has not—or at least not since Jefferson—had a high priest. It has not needed one. Man's natural attitude toward religion found no difficulty coming into confluence with the flow of national religion-in-general. Another way of saying this is that America has always been pluralist, doomed, or privileged, to work out its destiny on pluralist ground rules. But not until recent times has the enduring force of this pluralism been realized, and not until realized pluralism became the only option did the undue attachment to the assumption underlying it become obvious.

There are four major partners in the religious situation of today's America. Three of them—Protestants, Catholics, and Jews—go about their business in relatively peaceful coexistence. The fourth partner, however, is gaining, and at the expense of the other three, for he draws his recruits from among their members. What is more, the "convert" to the fourth partner may retain his membership in his original community of faith. The national religion thrives on "plural belonging." It makes fewer demands on potential converts and operates with an inner logic that defies massive refutation.

By way of introducing this fourth partner it is helpful to recall a parable that Will Herberg tells. The United States, he has argued, in its religious dimension did not represent a simple amalgam, one vast melting pot. Rather the rootless, alienated grandsons of immigrants found roots and a sense of belonging by identification with one of three clusters, found home in "return" to one of three melting pots. But only three. Herberg cites the army sergeant faced by a theologically precise recruit (was he Orthodox? High Anglican?) who refused to be classified as Protestant or Catholic or Jew. "Then what in blazes *are* you?" the sergeant bellowed.

The recruit might just as well have been theologically imprecise. Because there is a fourth pot that has no clear label. The "American" religious attitude, which Herberg describes as a product of the quest for belonging and the fruit of pluralism, is itself more and more assuming an *independent* position in American life. As it asserts its independence it contributes to the further skewing of that ancient relationship: Potestant majority, Roman Catholic, and Jewish minorities.

A seminar on religion in a free society planned by the Fund for the Republic in New York in May 1958 reckoned with this quadri-partite distinction. The seminar's chief importance, gathering as it did foremost figures associated with the question of church and state relations, lay in its celebration of realized pluralism. The keynote speaker was John Courtney Murray, who crystallized his remarks in a phrase about four extant "conspiracies." He used "conspiracy" without invidious connotation, as implying "united action for a common end about which there is agreement." The fourth conspiracy is most difficult to define. It has no pope or president or formal dogma. It lacks a name; the moment one names it one limits it. It includes elements of secularism, naturalism, nationalism, and humanism.

When this secular attachment to ultimacy takes shape as a religion it is protean, pervasive, persuasive. As Herberg has noted, it lives in the other groups but carries ambitions that overarch them all. Its maturation is bringing America into a situation in regard to religion much like that of Rome in the time of the Antonines, as reported by Gibbon:

The various modes of worship which prevailed in the Roman world were all considered by the people as equally true; by the philosopher as equally false; and by the magistrate as equally useful. And thus toleration produced not only mutual indulgence, but even religious concord.

However, since this religion has not yet fully conquered, we face, paradoxically, coexistent mutual indulgence and religious *discord*. Tensions have increased among formal professors of religion at a time when their commitment to the substance of individual faiths has lost its precision. The fourth religion has spread sufficiently and has plugged enough gaps that, in this quadri-conspiratorial sense, religion tabernacles almost suffocatingly over all citizens. There is no place else to go. It has become almost impossible for a man to be an infidel or even a dissenter.

Hence it is necessary to revise the time-honored terminology and to speak of a new religious establishment in America. It is a gradual growth that supplants the simple separation of church and state and the resultant religious voluntaryism that was the United States' outstanding institutional contribution to religious history. Custom and the compulsion of social pressures and national security have combined to forge this new establishment. Such compulsion is going to have to be countered by an alert and self-purifying pluralism in which committed Protestantism can play a significant part. Just what this new part should be is best determined by another rehearsal of its part in the past.

In most respects Protestantism has suffered more than the other conspirators. Its prior and larger investment made it more vulnerable. Its inner divisions rendered it less potent against massive erosion and occasional assault. The seeds of this suffering were planted in the American colonies from the first and they matured with the complication of varied immigration. Protestantism accepted without enthusiasm and sometimes with distaste the Roman Catholic and Jewish minorities as co-informers of the culture, but all along it coexisted with the nascent secular national religion that now is flowering. While Protestants pointed with pride to their achievements they hardly realized that the typically rationalist view of the irrelevancy of theological distinction in a pluralist society was pulling the rug out from under them. For a long time a Protestant majority gloried in its bluff, not noticing the winds which were eroding its position and its distinctiveness.

With the immigration to which we have referred went another complicating feature. This was the "diffusion of ideologies," to use Oscar Handlin's term, which accompanied later influxes of migrants. In the 1830s, says Handlin, there still existed a well-defined American ideology, compounded from the doctrines of the eighteenth-century Enlightenment, from the forms American religion took in its development from Calvinism, and from the terms in which the descendants of Europeans explained their contact with the wilderness. The ideology included some ideas of progress and perfectibility that were associated both with the men of the Enlightenment and with Arminian religion. During the next century 35 million immigrants arrived—Roman Catholicism and Judaism now acquiring sizable representation—who brought along different ideas and seemed less progressive, less optimistic, and this-worldly. Once the diffusion of these competing ideologies made its full effect felt it became obsolete to speak any longer of Protestant America, except in a disciplined historical sense. Since men in a time of diffusion of ideology need something at which to grasp, and since Protestantism was a particular option, it lost out to the less offensive general option. That meant, in Handlin's summary, that the Enlightenment prevailed over "the forms American religion took in its development from Calvinism."

The Protestant empire of which the Presbyterian historian Robert Baird spoke in the 1840s was now an authentically pluralistic society, though with considerable Protestant reminiscence. Long-time "minority" groups have found it profitable and advantageous to lengthen the shadow of Protestant prominence and provenance for strategic reasons. As late as 1927 foreign observers like André Siegfried could speak of Protestantism as the United States' "only national religion." They saw more the ancient stamp on the ethos than the immediate dynamics; Protestant chauvinists overstated their case and, as their position became weaker, shouted louder. But Protestant America is now as obsolete as the side-wheel showboat, the cigar-store Indian, or the Fourth of July oration. We all think of these as part of our culture—but where do we go to find them?

Whatever else it included, the "old shape" of American religion was basically Protestant.

Whatever else it includes, the "new shape" of American religion is not basically Protestant.

To be sure, I do not mean in this connection to bury a very live and growing institutional complex and theological emphasis. Protestantism is happily on the move even in the midst of its insecurities. I am arguing for a revised version of its destiny in pluralism America, to free it of nostalgia so that it can get to work with all its senses alert. When I speak here of post-Protestant America I mean only that its role as virtual monopolist in penetrating and molding the religious aspect of national culture has disappeared.

The statistics of the Protestant "conspiracy" are very encouraging. The *Yearbook of American Churches* for 1958 reported that in 1956, there were 60,148,980 Protestants to 34,563,851 Roman Catholics and 5,500,000 Jews. Even more inflated—as further substantiation of Herberg's "identification" thesis—is the projection of a study made by the Federal Bureau of the Census in March 1957 which would have 79 million Americans above the age of fourteen *thinking* of themselves as Protestants, to only 30,700,000 thinking of themselves as Catholics and 3,900,000 as Jews. On such a projection only 3,200,000 Americans would be listed as of no religion. Now (let us keep in mind all the inflation for which denominational statistics are notorious) Protestant churches claim but 60 million people of all ages, whereas, according to the census, almost 20 million more than that over the age of fourteen would list themselves as Protestant! Here is where the cutting edge of Protestantism is worn most dull. Here one would be likely to find the bulk of the supporters of the fourth conspiracy ("What in blazes *are* you?"), who are untrained in the use of proper terms for self-identification.

All the while, for over a century, Roman Catholicism has been carefully cultivating the picture of its minority status. When it breaks that pattern many are confused or enraged. Paul Hutchinson, when editor of *The Christian Century,* told of an incident that followed the late Cardinal Stritch's assertion that Protestantism is no longer the majority religion in this country. Hutchinson received indignant letters demanding that he rebuke the Cardinal and reassert "the fact that this is a Protestant nation." He did not because it was not. He did not—not because of the unreliability of statistics but because he recognized beyond statistics a change of status in urban and power centers as the background for new Catholic muscle-flexing. Anglo-American and Puritan-Protestant culture, if it is not being displaced, is at least merely coexisting as shaper of national customs. The dictator who asked, "How many legions has the pope?" was talking beside the point in our pluralistic culture. The Pope hardly need enter the picture and the Roman Catholic Church needs neither legions nor laws if it has suasion, custom, and success on its side.

While America by no means represents Roman Catholic culture, Catholicism can be used as an excellent illustration of how things have changed. Catholicism controls the urban centers with few exceptions outside the South and America is now a nation of urban dominance. Because of Protestantism's divisions, unassertiveness, and lack of symbolism, Catholicism tends to dominate the mass media. If Protestantism is represented in a motion picture or television drama it is usually only to the degree that it overlaps with the national religion-in-general. It must be inoffensive and inarticulate. Protestant clergymen are usually depicted as silver-haired smilers who preside at family rites and never say anything that is not innocuous. But Roman Catholic priests, from *Going My Way* to *On the Waterfront,* are real persons with authentic individuality. The Protestants may be "God's kind of guys" but the Catholics are men's kind of guys.

Newspaper coverage illustrates the metropolitan dominance of Roman Catholicism. One instance: The death of Samuel Cardinal Stritch got more Chicago newspaper lineage than did that of any political figure in memory. Hardly any Protestant leader's passing in the past five years was noted on the front page. Of course, Stritch ruled an archdiocese of 1.8 million Catholics, most of whom read newspapers. Complaints against the newspapers were unwarranted. They printed what sold. It is hardly necessary to comment on the space given the death of Pope Pius XII and the coronation of Pope John XXIII. Again, few subscriptions were canceled. The mass-media men know their audience. If an occasional Protestant, Jewish, or secularist voice complained about references in the press to Stritch as "our" Cardinal or Pius as "our" spiritual leader, the complaint was promptly rebuked in print by other Protestants, Jews, or secularists, for raising an intolerant point at a moment of tragedy.

Little wonder, then, that Protestantism is insecure in the face of this minority group's vital majority where it matters most. Catholicism has largely accepted responsibly its growing share in American culture. Its more grateful sons point to its profit from the pluralism which many have seen to be incompatible with its claims. But in such a constellation, when Protestants' insecurities cause them to strike out wildly or Catholics' embarrassments with their new virtual majorities cause them to act irresponsibly, new tensions will rise despite a growing apathy toward the substantive theology of each.

Jewish culture has come to take a similarly responsible place in political life, in the entertainment world, in literature and the arts, nearly controlling them in many urban centers. It is difficult to picture such Protestant domination of airwaves as marked the religio-national observance of the tenth anniversary of the founding of the State of Israel. Judaism gains and Christianity loses particularity at interfaith gatherings, where religious expression usually tends to sound Jewish because the "offense" of Christianity must be omitted, and as a courtesy according to the ground rules. The complaints on the part of Jews that their rights have been trampled on and their assumptions subsumed under a suffocating Christian overlay are certainly in place. The parallel complaints that they are insufficiently heard as a minority group are less warranted, if a statistical approach means anything.

Both illustrations suggest how Protestantism loses and will increasingly lose to the extent that mass media assist in informing American culture in its religious dimension as well as in others. This is part of the price Protestantism must now pay for having informed American culture. In the course of the long hearing granted it, Protestantism often neglected to show that evangelicalism and Americanism were not the same thing. Now, other portrayals of Americanism are claiming "equal time." The reunion of the churches and the recovery of theological depth among Protestants may prove a partial diversion from the one-way flow of this stream.

Since in the situation of realized pluralism we have agreed to play the game with four participants, it can be expected that they will be given handicaps so that their contributions will be virtually equal no matter what their size or heritage. Or, to change the picture, the pourings from four melting pots—whatever their relative size—into the mainstream of American national culture on a virtually equal basis is too familiar a phenomenon to require documentation. What is more elusive is the specific identification and shape of the crystallizing secular tradition that is becoming the fourth religion.

What name shall it have? At the New York seminar referred to above, John Courtney Murray spoke of secular humanism as a latecomer, profiting from the religious molding of Western culture. But in America it was actually an early comer, that nameless analogy ("Deism" is too precise) to the European Enlightenment which is associated with our national fathers. Its organized and institutional forms ("Republican Religion," one historian called it) were swept aside in the revivals of the first half of the nineteenth century. Its secular individualistic activism was content to coexist in quiescence or in co-operation with religious optimism. Only after the full effect of competition among religious absolutes made itself felt, when the age of immigration had ended and in a time of national insecurity and the quest for an ideology, did it bloom again. That time came only recently, and we in the churches have not yet learned to deal with this flowering.

One thing many Protestants undertook was to clip the flowers and press them in their own albums. There has been a broad attempt at rewriting the tradition in Christian terms. Popular magazines and pulpits of the most orthodox Christian cast resort every February to attempts at proving that Washington and Lincoln were conventional and orthodox Christians. Washington found a broad Episcopalian way of life congenial to his broader religious philosophy; Lincoln made it quite clear that he was not at home in conventional Christian churches. But they are the saints of the national religion, and Protestants like to enthrone them in their own hagiology. More sophisticated commentators have fallen into a similar error. Perry Miller was correct when he pointed out in a book review that the founding fathers were of a "liberality" of spirit which must forever and properly remain a scandal to the rank and file of professing American Christians.

But in recent years definition has become more precise. The phenomenon is becoming isolated for what it is, a secular religion coexisting with the other three conspiracies. Eugene Carson Blake when president of the National Council of Churches in 1955 spoke of "America's humanistic nationalism" as an ideology in competition for the American heart and mind. He outlined only the cruder form of a complex phenomenon that we shall be called to dissect; but as far as it goes his description is helpful.

> This ideology is what an American is if nobody tampers with his attitudes. His articles of faith are science (in its engineering applications), common sense (his own ideas), the Golden Rule (in its negative form), sportsmanship, and individual independence. . . . I have called this a humanism not because he doesn't believe in God. He does, but his god is not to be confused with a transcendent being to whom he owes duty and life itself, but rather his god is a combination of whipping boy, servant and even a useful ally in dealing with religious people, who otherwise might get in his way.

This ideology in its refined form, which is as much different from what Blake describes as Reinhold Niebuhr is from Protestant hill-country rollers and shouters, must now be provided for in symposia along with the *other* three religions. Examples: the Fund for the Republic seminar; a study by Protestants, Jews and secularists of the Roman Catholic Church; the ginger-and-gentility attitude which representatives of the other three religions exhibited toward this fourth approach to ultimacy in the discussion of "Secular Images of Man" at the Religious Education Association meeting in Chicago, December 1957; the book *Patterns of Faith in America Today,* which, along with essays on the three conventional religions, presents a study of "naturalistic humanism" by John Herman Randall, Jr. Randall's response to the compulsion to be identified religiously in the situation of "establishment by mores" is clear. He speaks for the "fellow-travelers of religion," "sensitive and thoughtful men [who] share a concern with the part religion plays in human life" but are not content with its forms.[1] Likewise the altar to the unknown God received its incense in Leo Rosten's *Look* magazine series of 1955 (later published in book form as *A Guide to the Religions of America*). To fill in the gaps after reporting most religious groups of size and interest, Rosten asked ethical culturist Jerome Nathanson to speak for the "sixty-four million Americans [who] do not go to church." Nathanson's most important lines, suggesting a fourth category of belonging: these 64 million Americans "share an important attitude—the idea that it is possible to be 'religious,' moral, decent, without joining a group and worshipping *en masse*. They believe the individual can get as close to the idea of God as any cleric or institution can bring him."[2] Almost none of them are *anti*religious, Nathanson hastens to point out. But unfortunately there is no label for this 64-million-member "minority"; no one speaks for them. "We must remember that when the 'three faiths' have expressed themselves, we have not canvassed all sides of religious and moral questions." Precisely. "How many legions has the pope?" Certainly not 64 million fellow shapers of American destiny. We can agree with Professor Arthur Mann of Massachusetts Institute of Technology in his discussion of the "Religion of Democracy" in *Commentary:*

> What the Deists hoped to achieve without a church has in large degree come to pass in the land of many churches. Indeed, the idea that religion is handmaiden to democracy has made such headway that *American Catholicism, American Protestantism, and American Judaism appear like parallel shoots on a common stock.* [Italics mine.][3]

Democracy becomes the ultimate, religion the handmaiden.

If this is the implicit faith of most Americans it is the explicit faith of some of them. It has an impressive cluster of spokesmen. While analysis of the writings of the Niebuhrs or the Maritains may not be the best way of going about studying Protestantism or Catholicism, it is at least *a* way of beginning. While analysis of the declarations of the sophisticates of this surrogate for religion may not be the best way of going about studying it, we can begin here. And we can, though very timidly, give the emphasis a name: "The Religion of Democracy." The term crops up again and again in the writings of its professors and its critics. It bears no invidious connotation. It is sufficiently imprecise to be inclusive, and sufficiently narrow to exclude the "three great faiths."

Let me cite but three of the apologists for "The Religion of Democracy": the late A. Powell Davies, a liberal clergyman from Washington who defended its spirit; Mrs. Agnes Meyer, journalist and educator who has pointed to its battleground; Professor J. Paul Williams, who has worked toward its refinement. Dozens of others could be cited, but these three are representative.

If we are accustomed to begin a review of another religion by examining its dogma, we shall be hard put in this instance. The religion of democracy relies to a large extent on the untranscribed consensus which makes a free and pluralistic society possible. But it elevates that broad consensus to ultimacy. Hence one can hardly expect a clear theological statement from this secular and humanistic faith. It solicits devotion and feeling and refinement of attitude toward the free society. What is sought parallels what someone described as President Eisenhower's spiritual expression: "a very fervent faith in a very vague religion."

From time to time men set out to articulate the consensus, to give it substance. A. Powell Davies was one of these. An unrepentant liberal, he liked to speak of the religion of democracy as "America's real religion." It has been suggested that reading him would convince the doubter that Washington, Jefferson, and other founding fathers believed thoroughly in this religion of democracy. In his book *Man's Vast Future* Davies makes a formal attempt to define "Democracy as a Faith." His definition is typical, comprehensive, and probably acceptable to the majority of the faith's adherents:

The democratic faith is a belief that man, if he resolves upon it, can raise the level of his life indefinitely, making the world increasingly more happy, more just, and more good; no fate has made him prisoner of his circumstances, no natural weakness has condemned him to be ruled by tyranny. He is meant to be free. Through the power of reason he can form intelligent opinions, and by discussion and definition can test them, knowing that truth is precious above all things and the only safe guide to purposes and aims, the right to seek it must be held inviolate.

And the democratic faith declares that human rights are by their nature universal, that liberty is such a right, and that without liberty there cannot be justice; that to ensure justice, the people should make the laws under which they live; that besides justice there should be benevolence and sympathy, that those doctrines of religion which beseech mankind to practice brotherhood are right; that love must expel hate, and good will take the place of malice; that as well as zeal there must be patience and forbearance, and that persuasion is better than coercion; that none should hold the people in contempt, or profane the sacredness of conscience, or deny the worth of human life; and finally, that God and history are on the side of freedom, justice, love, and righteousness, and man will therefore, be it soon or late, achieve a world society of peace and happiness where all are free and none shall be afraid.[4]

A fine statement, and a familiar creed. Superimposed as a political view on a foundation of other religions, it would be most acceptable. But what is significant about it is its reach: this is to be the religious foundation; particularity is unimportant if not actually obstructive. Davies made that repeatedly clear.

This is not, of course, a new creed; it has only recently come to status. Out of an embarrassment of riches, hear the expression of a liberal churchman, Rabbi Charles Fleischer, at the turn of the century: "We of America are the 'peculiar people' consecrated to that 'mission' of realizing Democracy [which] is potentially a universal spiritual principle, aye, a religion . . . men like Washington, Samuel Adams, Jefferson, Lincoln [should be] placed literally in a calendar of saints to be reverenced by our future Americans as apostles of our Republic." What this churchman said should be, has been done.

A religion to be strong must be militant. It must feel itself embattled, must have some sort of crusade. That the religion of democracy faces ideological contests on a world-wide level is obvious; and in these contests it is joined by the other three great faiths. But on the domestic level it faces the problem of ensuring its own propagation. It has few temples or churches or synagogues. But it has an "established church" in the field of public education. In the face of those who suggest that public education should be neutral or noncommittal in the matter of religion, its supporters urge that it teach this specific profession. They are most disturbed by sectarian intrusions on the line separating church and state. Here, evidently, is to be the battle line in the years ahead.

In this front line Mrs. Agnes Meyer, wife of the publisher of *The Washington Post,* has been a most eloquent spokesman.[5] For her, John Dewey is "the most religious of contemporary thinkers." Her ideological roots are in the Locke-Jefferson religious tradition. But not only does what she sees as America's "liberal" past serve as a ground of faith: so conservative a document as the Constitution is "anything but irreligious."

[It has] positive views on the subject of religion . . . preserving and carrying over into the secular realm much of the idealism which had been identified with religion . . . a specifically Christian philosophy that can never be lost is closely interwoven with its principles, and with our democratic thought and action.

Mrs. Meyer has declared herself in agreement with Henry Steele Commager's view that "public education has become the American religion. . . . The schools are the noblest manifestation of the religion of the Constitution, and are by no means 'Godless' as contemporary ecclesiastical critics would have us believe." Such noble institutions are worthy of noble defense. Mrs. Meyer proclaims that "the secular tolerance of religious diversity . . . alone makes brotherhood possible in our country."

This spiritual unity is the saving grace of democracy and its real defense against totalitarianism or against the divisive influence of sectarianism. Therefore what can justly be called the unifying mission of secularism has a sanctity all its own. Rightly understood and valued, secularism will accelerate its Christian democratic mission to make us all brothers of one another.

When we realize, moreover, that the Public School is the chief vehicle for mutual love, forgiveness, and tolerance between all races, classes, and creeds, it becomes an act of vandalism to attack it and an act of piety to work toward its improvement.

On this premise she has attacked the impious "medieval-minded clergy" with their "outworn authoritarian verbalism." Religious differences are trivial:

The school needs all of its time to improve the education of our children and to center upon the task of developing the morality and strength of character that are ideals common to men of all religious faiths. . . . the secularization of the schools was a positive movement to embody in American education the interaction of the real and the ideal, upon which both democracy and active Christianity depend. Whenever a human being strives upward for self-development, goodness, and concern for others, there the divine will is active. . . . Democracy can generate a system of moral principles . . . a secular morality.

The Commonweal was quick to pick up this defense when it first appeared and to nominate Mrs. Meyer *the* national spokesman of "democracy as a religion, or a substitute for religion, a rival to religion, or [a reduction of] religion to the role of its political handmaiden." It is not hard to see why. It recognized thoughtful-

ness, seriousness, coherence, sincerity. But it also saw the danger
that befalls when democracy exists in order to answer "the ultimate
why's" and the public schools become its seminaries. Mrs. Meyer's
views have found considerable consent and support. Whoever
wishes to see this emergent faith in action will see it best in the
battle for the schools.

It remains, then, only to find someone capable of making this
faith explicit, dogmatic, and ceremonial. Perhaps no such prophet
has appeared, but he has an eloquent forerunner in the person of
Professor J. Paul Williams of Mount Holyoke College. During the
height of America's revival of interest in religion Williams wrote
a book whose general tenor seemed to be typical of religion-in-
general. But *What Americans Believe and How They Worship*[6]
"unfortunately had a thesis," as one reviewer put it. The thesis appeared in the concluding chapter, "The Role of Religion in Shaping
American Destiny." This provides chilling bedtime reading for
traditional Christians, especially if one agrees with Professor James
Hastings Nichols that "Professor Williams' program has perhaps an
even chance of succeeding, at least so far as a state religion is concerned." The chapter would be a good starting point for anyone
who needs to be awakened from dogmatic slumber.

Williams there argues that Americans do not have enough faith,
courage, and stamina to preserve what democracy they possess, let
alone to gain more and to play a democratic role on the world
stage. He has a program: Americans must come to look on the
democratic ideal "as the Will of God, or, if they please, the Law of
Nature . . . democracy must become an object of religious dedi-
cation." Churches and synagogues, whose current teachings are
harmless alternative symbols for universal needs, ought to teach
democracy as religion, as ultimate metaphysical truth. But they
are limited in reach and understanding. Therefore governmental
agencies must teach the democratic ideal *as religion*. For governmental agencies reach all citizens, and "systematic and universal
indoctrination is essential." Williams, too, turns eventually to the
schools because they are in the most strategic position to arouse
religious devotion for democracy. Schools now treat democracy as
an item of *religious* faith only accidentally and unsystematically.
They need to stress two new elements.

One is *metaphysical sanctions,* "open indoctrination of the faith that the democratic ideal accords with ultimate reality . . . that democracy is the very Law of Life." Embarrassed at the present vagueness of this creed Williams urges that people live according to it before they formulate it more precisely, for premature formulation might evoke "the specters of the naturalist-supernaturalist debate."

The other necessary element is *ceremonial reinforcement,* which would recall and glorify the set of values believed to have metaphysical sanction; self-appraisal in light of those values; and re-dedication to living according to the standards sanctioned by those values, to produce a "devotion to democratic ideals like the devotion given by ardent believers in every age to the traditional religious."

Williams finds company among our top educators and researchers as cited in the report of the second conference in "The Scientific Spirit and Democratic Faith." This report breathes the same air while attacking other authoritarianisms. The view of the conferees is summarized in a remark on the last page:

A working democracy would be modern religion at work. . . . If we really set to work to integrate the values which we recognize as democratic values in life, we will have done the religious job.

This makes explicit the kind of implicit faith President Eisenhower was assuming during his early years in office. If we arrange in sequence a variety of the President's utterances, a similiar creed emerges:

I believe in democracy.
A democracy cannot exist without a religious base.
Free government is the expression of a deeply felt religious faith.
You cannot simply explain free government in any other terms than religious.
This is the faith that teaches us all that we are children of God.
This faith teaches us that our ideals of democracy and freedom . . . are eternal laws of the human spirit.
The founding fathers wrote this religious faith into our founding documents . . . they put it squarely at the base of our institutions.
Happily our people have always reserved their first allegiance to the kingdom of the spirit.
America is the mightiest power which God has yet seen fit to put upon his footstool.
America is great because she is good.

The President, of course, is the President of all the people. Whatever his private faith, we do not expect him to profess a particular creed in his public utterances. But confusion enters in when church people fail to recognize that this overarching public expression is not a witness to God who is the Father of Jesus Christ, but a witness to God who is the Father of Demos—the democratic spirit of a nation. There is a difference.

When we examine the Davies-Meyer-Williams formalization or the Eisenhower informalization of this faith, several critical questions come to mind. What are the alternatives that face an evangelical Christian?

Perhaps the spokesmen are wrong. Perhaps this is not a historic faith. Perhaps its prophets today and their predecessors in earlier crises just invented it to meet certain needs, and their appeals to the founding fathers are baseless and inaccurate.

Or: Perhaps it is a historic faith, but a dead one. Perhaps the fathers did propound such a view, valid for their day but not for ours—a view that should be abandoned as obsolete and inadequate.

Or: Perhaps it is the historic faith of some of the fathers, of the Jeffersonian type, but its prophets in their rewriting of Jefferson overrate its total importance. The extremely significant nonconformist-Puritan tradition in American religion and the national past, for example, may balance or cancel it. What was the Church in times past saying of this religion of democracy?

Or: Perhaps it is a historic faith which does not or need not concern Christians in the middle of the twentieth century. Simply to recognize that it is or was an ideology would then be enough.

Or: Perhaps it is a historic faith that can be countered through theological criticism, review, and reconstruction.

My own answer would be something on this line: The spokesmen of the "Religion of Democracy" school are reaching for and appropriating an authentic parcel of the American past. They are more accurate in their reading of the founding fathers than are the unthinking Christians who try to make Protestants out of them and who try to theologize all the basic documents or our national history on Christian lines. They are taking aspects of a consensus which the "three great faiths" support and elevating them to ultimacy. They have a right to their expression, and their expression is certainly preferable to antireligious alternatives.

But their expression is something quite different from the Christian faith, and until Christians recognize this they will contribute to further erosion of the vital edges of their own witness. They will welcome spokesmen of this fourth conspiracy as partners in support of the national consensus, but *not* as allies in witness to God the Father of Jesus Christ, the God of the Christian faith. In short, they will recognize the spokesmen of the fourth conspiracy as conspirators, and will resist their efforts to establish their version of the democratic creed as the official American faith.

If my reading of the situation is accurate, it is clear such resistances are not now occurring on any large scale. Instead, Arthur Mann's dictum seems to be true: "American Catholicism, American Protestantism, and American Judaism appear like parallel shoots on a common stock," a form of nationalism. (We are, let us recall, discussing the new shape of *American* religion and dealing with America as a whole.) Jacques Maritain, in a pleasant-humored Valentine to America, treated this danger. The religious inspiration at work in the temporal consciousness of America, he wrote, is rooted in particular religious creeds to which the various citizens subscribe. But this religious inspiration in the *collective* behavior of the nation tends to become a projection of religious belief *into the temporal order.*

Just as it is not particularly favorable, as a rule, for religion to be too much brandished about and made use of by the officials of any government, so the much deeper phenomenon of which I just spoke—temporalized religious inspiration in a nation or a civilization—however normal and salutary it may be in itself, involves its own accidental dangers. The risk is that *religion itself* might become temporalized, in other words, so institutionalized in the temporal structures themselves and the temporal growth itself of a given civilization, that it would practically lose its essential supernatural, supra-temporal, and supranational transcendence, and become subservient to particular national or temporal interests.[7]

Maritain quotes Barbara Ward:

It is one thing to argue that a recovery of faith in God is necessary as a safeguard of Western freedom. It is quite another to put forward sociological and political and historical facts as the basis for a revival of faith. . . . Faith is not a matter of convenience nor even—save indirectly—a matter of sociology. . . . Faith will not be restored in the West because people believe it to be useful. It will return only when they find that it is true.

In other words, Maritain adds, we do not need a faith to live by; we need a faith to live for and, if necessary, to die for.

Let us say, then, that any temporalized religious inspiration runs the risk of terminating in a failure if religion in its own order does not victoriously resist any trend toward becoming itself temporalized, that is to say, if, in the inner realm of human souls, faith in supernatural Truth and obedience to the law of God, the fire of true love and the life of divine grace are not steadily growing.

✶ I have argued here that what Maritain sees as a risk has become a reality for millions of Americans: the fourth conspiracy represents the temporalization of religion in the democratic structures.

Until it is recognized as a fourth faith, a vague and somewhat sentimental religious syncretism that will do small service to healthy pluralistic dialogue is bound to increase in influence and favor. Introduction of the term "syncretism" at this point is not intended to cloud the issue: it says exactly what should be said. Syncretism can mean two things, following two etymologies. According to Plutarch, the term derives from the fact that the Cretans, though they disputed and fought among themselves, repeatedly united to fight off enemies of their island. This form of syncretism, a temporary, pragmatic, terms-understood coexistence and alliance, can be creative, assuming as we must within the religious community that what our "Cretan brothers" are arguing about is of ultimate concern. The other form of syncretism, which has a hazy etymology implying a mixing together of religions, is not creative. It produces a hybrid faith. It is unfaithful to man's higher visions and responses to the call for truth. Yet this "amiable syncretism" as we see it in suburban life (the phrase is Riesman's) is most widespread. Living-room Deism has its day: We have all heard its universal and corrosive credo: "After all, we're simply in different boats heading for the same shore."

No minister would be hard put to document the corrosiveness of this creed in the lives of his members. A preacher may spend years enunciating a faith with precision and perhaps even with a false sense of exclusiveness. Yet he will hear the members of his own audience bounce back with generalized syncretistic utterances. The slogan about different boats heading for the same shore was once wafted my way by a Roman Catholic civic leader of the newer suburban ethos, not two minutes after he had reproved me for contradicting his church's dogmatic teaching. I had applied the term "Protestant" to a lapsed Catholic now worshiping as a Protestant: "You're wrong there. If they get that water of baptism on them, they're Catholic until the day they die!" This clash between dogma intellectually held and ethos emotionally recognized is sharpened to the degree that American Protestants, Catholics, and Jews unwittingly and uncritically support their fourth conspiratorial partner.

When national or local community ultimates rob religions of their valid particularity, the fourth overarching conspiracy becomes overpowering and the other three become progressively irrelevant and impotent. Thus an intuitive quasi-religious American way of life with a sort of state Shinto has developed. What has brought about this state of affairs—this amiable syncretism *coexisting* with unamiable intergroup tensions? Why are conflicts between faiths growing at the very time when the substantive position of each is held with less passion?

The reason, I would suggest, is a combination of several factors: the insecurity of Protestantism as it recognizes the *fait accompli* of its new "minority" status; the minority complex with quasi-majority responsibility of Roman Catholicism; the quest for definition by Judaism; and the confusion of all three in the presence of the secular, national, natural, humanistic, religion of democracy. What is the way out? Our hope lies in pragmatic, terms-understood cooperation and in a decrease of tension which can come only as each conspiracy re-evaluates its potential contribution to the pluralistic life in what Albert Camus calls *"la civilisation du dialogue."* It is at this point that we must call upon a sense of history, sincerity, charity, and commitment to truth. For only then, as majorities shift, will new majorities refrain from vindictiveness against those they have displaced. Here we must learn from the American experience and draw upon the riches of the inherited intuitive wisdom of the people, rather than spend energy hardening new ideologies of democratic life.

What legacy does Protestantism bring to the new dialogue? We have said that, taking America as a whole, it is no longer possible to speak of its Puritan-Protestant or Anglo-American ethos in a pervasive sense. When people speak out of the remaining Anglo-American outposts, or out of the Midwestern rural communities still shaped by religious groups of Continental Protestant provenance, they are talking about a situation which is rapidly dissolving because of population mobility and the impact of mass media.

The achievement of Protestantism in shaping our culture and national life is impressive. No significant and plausible detraction from this obvious fact by members of the other three conspiracies has yet been made. To call this a post-Protestant culture is to pay it the compliment of historical reference and deference. But the "post-" is as important as the enduring "Protestant" in the phrase. We must ask what substantive, positive, Protestant contribution is active today in shaping America as a whole.

What most people mean when they speak of this contribution is something negative: the blue-nose, blue-law "Puritan" outlook which never even existed among the Puritans. This idea is relatively meaningless for several reasons. Protestantism's inner life is complicated by various ethical patterns. Much of the ascetic Protestant impulse that found its way into legislation was a late and often accidental addition to the central Protestant thrust. Perhaps the most important contribution that critical and prophetic Protestantism can now make is hearty participation out of its own ultimate commitments in the dialogue. It can contribute out of its own resource toward an understanding of the ground rules of dialogue. For Protestantism insists that it has "truth," but that the truth man possesses is partial. If, as old John Robinson said to the Puritans in a phrase that their descendants relish, God has more truth and light to break forth from His holy word—*then,* confident in that word and humbled by the fact that "now we know in part and prophesy in part," Protestants should delight in the dialogue and contend for the creative possibilities of authentic pluralism.

In this spirit they must vigorously rebel against the new establishment, against the official sanctioning of an attitude toward the religion of democracy or realized pluralism in general. They represent an ethos that would allow for no escape, no dissent. However heartily they support toleration as an attitude, Protestants must reject it as an exhaustive religious category. Here the centrifugal sects of "Third Force Christendom," the protesting intransigents, may be of some help. The square pegs that do not fit the round holes of eroded religious expression might call us all to a higher witness. But continued atheological expressions of an imposed common national faith to which so many Protestants, Catholics, and Jews are already committing themselves, are more likely to cloud and blur their contributions. In any case, such expressions are largely unnecessary in an America which has muddled through quite well without articulating universally acceptable ideologies.

Necessary agreements there are, no doubt, in that inherited intuitive wisdom of the people, in the broad ideas that have made our pluralistic society possible and healthy. But to ask participants in the dialogue to formulate and articulate and accept these, to desert their diversities and obscure their particularities, will only enhance the new establishment at the expense of the religious vitality of the individual conspiracies. Simple chumminess, whether imposed by national compulsion or generated by amiable syncretism, if it asks the price of commitment to truth as ticket to the arcades and temples of national religion, is dangerous. To change the metaphor: its warmth may yet melt the melting pots so that their vital contents spill out. That is not what dialogue is all about.

Meanwhile, Protestants can enter the dialogue with less anxiety over their status by admitting frankly the new facts of life. Nostalgia here is unproductive. Yearning for the golden age of evangelical triumph in America overlooks the effects of immigration, secularization, urbanization. Participants in a dialogue should not have to be nudged repeatedly to be awakened out of a dream world. In this new quadri-conspiratorial constellation, Protestantism, in the interests of truth and strategy, should begin to learn to enjoy the luxury and to work with the reality of its minority status in a pluralistic post-Protestant culture.

Five

The Setting for the Future: Panurbia

THE NEW shape of American religion arises not only from an erosion of Protestant particularity in its views of God, man, and community, but also from a complication of milieu. On the national level religion-in-general, realized pluralism, and a religion of democracy have graduated into the status Protestantism once held. Many church people today are hardly conscious of church work on a national level. To them, the local parochial unit represents the Church. It fights the Church's battles, carries its Cross, and rejoices in its victories in the local situation. For that reason an assessment of the prospects of the churches requires a look at the varying dimensions of change in those local situations.

But before exploring "local situations" to determine their drama and their power, let us review the recent past in the light of the longer perspective. My habit of reviewing leaves us teetering on the edge of tomorrow, for while clues from the past may give us a general sense of direction for the future, the variety and unpredictability of American life makes any sort of specific prophecy hazardous. To take one instance: no doubt the most dramatic change in the situation of man in the later 1950s was brought about through his entrance into the space age. This enlargement of horizons will almost certainly have a profound effect on religious life among the people on the earthward side of a launching pad.

All of us, however, would probably be at a complete loss to

predict the nature of that effect. America's recovery of initiative in scientific matters may work to embolden the nation and induce a new era of pride. Such a development could be accompanied by a relative indifference to religion—man grows, God is dethroned. Or it might work the opposite way. The shrinking of man in the universe and his bewilderment as he arrives at new scientific frontiers may cause greater anxieties and promote a more fevered quest for God. Or the very pace of change may dull our collective perceptions and make us apathetic. Nor do these exhaust the possibilities.

The only thing we can say with some assurance is this: As satellites swirl and America enters the space age, our more speculative analysts will have cause to measure the cost in new psychic damage to the men and women of the latter part of the twentieth century. And this change in outlook is certain to have some sort of effect on religion. Not often in the history of the race has there been as dramatic and sudden a change in its relation to the physical universe as we have experienced since World War II. But all this is nothing that might be of use in planning for the future.

Meanwhile such speculation distracts from some of the planning which must be done by realistic church people who are concerned with the propagation of the Christian Gospel. While we have our noses off in space and our minds on an unknown future, documentable changes of first significance are going on right under them. These changes can be evaluated in the light of the past. In other words, we can take our bearings and establish a sense of direction. We can even gather resources for re-evaluating strategy to deal with the changes.

The change that, insofar as it affects American religion, stands out above all others is the social revolution connected with urbanization—the maturation and culmination of a century-long process whose psychic and spiritual effects are now for the first time being fully realized for America as a whole. We shall consider this phenomenon from the viewpoint of concerned Protestantism. In more respects than one America is becoming, perhaps has already become, entirely urban in its outlook. The rural ethos is now an isolated and waning force. Everything is city; "panurbia" is here. This is the most dramatic challenge presented to Protestant ingenuity in America since, over a century ago, the churches had to learn to adjust to the principle of voluntaryism for support.

At first glance it would seem that the total urbanization of America or of any country can have nothing more than a superficial connection with the Christian prospect. "God was in Christ reconciling the world unto himself"—the directness of this Good News is universal in its intent. Theoretically, it should make little difference where men are or how they are situated when this news is proclaimed to them. Yet even within Christendom and even within a Christian civilization, huge clusters of people are situated in places that seem to make them unreachable by the Gospel or to make its proclamation relatively meaningless. If the churches are bewildered by the problem it is not because the factors that produce it are remote but because they are so near.

It is this nearness that causes difficulty for the writer too. One can speak with detachment and authority of religious affairs in realms remote in time or space. But when one deals with data near at hand and in the present he is himself involved, and he begins with a type of documentation which can be handled with equal authority by most of his contemporaries. Nevertheless, we shall labor the obvious in this chapter. For though the facts of urban change are plain to see, it remains true that Protestants are only beginning to learn to cope with them. My object then is neither to prophesy nor to pontificate but to place in context the kind of changes in national life which affect religious life and witness.

Let us begin with a contrast to our glamorous but rather useless illustration from outer space. The new shape of American religion is being molded by much more easily documentable physical and psychic changes on the less-out-of-reach plane of interpersonal relations in "urbia" today. Here the space age means that with the closing of the frontier and the growth of population and horizontal mobility, we have been running out of space. Religious and ethnic groups, long in isolation, are now fluid and can no longer depend upon distance from competitors and definition of boundaries for the strength of their own existence.

Panurbia can be seen and described in two ways. The first is diagrammatic: take out a map and a book of statistics and chart it with arrows and lines of flow and graphs. This is the physical change from the time when America could be pictured as an agrarian nation with several growing urban centers to the new panurban situation. The second way is dialogic. Conversation crosses the boundaries of urban and lately rural areas. There is psychic violation of remaining boundaries between farm, village, suburb, and metropolis particularly by the mass media of communication. Movies, radios, television, mass-circulation magazines, and newspapers are generally planned for all America, and thus they tend to homogenize cultures largely according to the urban norms where they originate. In both the physical and psychic dimensions religion is affected. It is not at all difficult to show how profoundly Protestantism is involved in the change.

Were I to preach a sermon on this subject, the text would come from a passing sentence of Paul Hutchinson.

"Well, urban civilization is not Protestant."

Note well, this sentence does not say it *cannot* be Protestant— only that it is not. To amplify:

> Our cities have been great catch-alls for immigration, and most of that has not been Protestant. Moreover, rural dwellers who move to the cities and go into our gigantic factories and mills, while living in the rabbit warrens of our apartment house districts, often lose touch with the church. . . . American culture, in this urbanized period into which we have moved, is no longer Protestant. It has never been, and is not now, Roman Catholic. It is not religious at all. We still like to employ religious symbols, but actually we are now living in a secular culture. Secularism has taken over in the United States.[1]

In place of "secularism" I should prefer "generalized religion," but for the rest I would agree. Well, at least urban civilization is not Protestant. This is a commonplace, a virtually universal observation. A person must be of extremely provincial orientation and his vision must be limited to what he can see from his own church balcony if he believes otherwise.

Evangelical Christianity seemed to nurture and, reciprocally, to thrive on rural culture. It was unable to absorb nineteenth-century immigration, which concentrated in cities. It was organizationally and often emotionally or spiritually unequipped to participate in urban dynamics.

However, identifications and limitations need not circumscribe Protestantism's participation in the life of today's panurbia or mar its hopes for the future. Always adaptive and sometimes creative, Protestantism has already shown signs here and there of urban awakening. A vital beginning awaits still wider recognition and comprehension of the new facts of life. On the new treadmill or escalator the facts of life are complicated in *Through the Looking Glass* fashion: "Now here, you see, it takes all the running you can do to keep in the same place. If you want to get somewhere else, you must run at least twice as fast as that." D. W. Brogan has remarked that long-term impacts of the discovery of atomic fission "are not so important . . . as some changes in the American way and the American view of life." "There are material changes," he said, "of which the most striking is the 'nationalization' of American life. . . . Over all the forty-eight states a new urbanized, highly mechanized, materially sophisticated culture has spread . . . a new America is being made."[2]

The first fact one must face in a review of this type is the population explosion. Even if we allow for a wider use of birth-control devices, it is not likely that the predictions which point to a national population of 300 million by the turn of the century are entirely out of line. In the past such predictions have fallen notably short. For example, in 1946 the Bureau of the Census predicted a population of 150 million by 1955. It fell short by almost 17 million in the nine-year span—an error of forecasting that represented more than Canada's entire population. No matter what tapering occurs in the rate of growth, the fact remains that all trends point toward a crowding United States. And it is the cities that are growing fastest. We shall not, in the next years, be crowding one another off the map, but we shall have to learn to live in closer proximity to our neighbors. In 1950 83.8 million people lived in Standard Metropolitan Areas; in 1956, 96.2 million lived in them. Growth in Standard Metropolitan Areas is four times as rapid as it is in nonmetropolitan areas. Meanwhile, what happens to the farm?

During the 1950s, 450–500 fewer people lived in rural America every day of every year. Urbanization by subtraction is limiting the potency of the rural ethos in the United States. Not only the historical connection with Protestantism but the closeness to creation, the intimacy of personal relations, the relative simplicity of ethical situations in a man-to-man world predisposed churches toward success in rural America. A. M. Schlesinger, Sr., has spoken of the myth of the "long tutelage of the soil" as the chief formative influence which produced courage, creative energy, and resourcefulness along with independence, homely ingenuity, and capacity for work. All of this, when informed by evangelicalism, produced what we have called Arminian man. The new post-Arminian man is under different influence.

In so far as universals can be found in life and character in America, they are due less to any common tutelage of the soil than to the leveling influence of urban civilization, and above all, to the standardization of the big technology and of the media of mass communication.[3]

This means that any religious movement or denomination dependent largely on the farm shrinks as rural life shrinks. On October 19, 1957, the Federal Bureau of the Census reported a drop of 1,861,000 in the farm population during the year April 1956 to April 1957. Every eleventh farm dweller had sold his tractor and moved to the city or else was absorbed by the pavements of sprawling urbia, "one of the largest [changes] ever recorded." Between 1950 and April 1957 farm population decreased by 4,700,000 down to 20,396,000 men, women, and children, while the total population increased more than 19 million.

Farm mechanization requires fewer workers; job opportunities elsewhere beckon. Twelve per cent of the population lived on farms in April 1957 as against 17 per cent in 1950. The Department of Agriculture reports a 17 per cent decline in the number of farms in the United States in a decade. Contrast the one-eighth of the population now engaged in agricultural production with the one-half so engaged in 1880 and the three-quarters in 1820 and one begins to realize the strength of the urban magnet. The future? In an address as president of the American Economic Association (and, by the way, as a defender of the family farm) John D. Black projected an America with four million farms and a total farm labor force of five million in 1975.

None of this need be marked as tragedy. The number of farms is declining not simply because of the attractions of the cities but because labor-saving devices and technological change have made it unnecessary for half the population to farm to feed the other half. But if it is not tragedy, it is still change and must be recognized as such. Farms are becoming larger and cities and suburbs more compressed; hence the continuing spatial illusion of persisting rural strength. But the creative rural church movement in the United States is not numbed by the illusion. It knows the difficulty of the work ahead as rural Protestantism declines in mid-twentieth-century power structures. It knows the insecurities that many farmers experience as their place in American life seems less and less sure.

Mark Rich, an eloquent spokesman for the rural church movement, sees hope in this realism and alertness: "The movement grew out of an awareness of the breakdown of the rural church. Impending disaster to rural institutions and to rural civilization was once heralded, and even now there are many pressing problems." But "rural life leaders today envision a strong church in town and country."[4] They envision this strong church because of their realism and because they have desentimentalized rural church talk. They carry a continuing sense of mission to a perpetual American minority. Most of all because of the application of specifically *urban* techniques (in the sense that they were learned and nurtured away from town and country) to rural church life, they are able to serve where they are.

These urban techniques include the use of sociological concepts learned from urban ecology, streamlined communication methods, dependence upon relations to secular community agencies, promotion of awareness of rural people's stake in world affairs, and a stress on the interlocking character of human life that, with pan-urbanization, is increasingly recognized. Meanwhile the New American has appeared on the farm also, for most of the technological devices that produced the lonely crowd in the cities and many of the institutional features that produced organization men in suburbia are producing both on farms.

From time to time I have compared notes on this change with other people of rural background who have lived in metropolitan areas much of their lives. Most of us carry in our minds an image of the farm of the recent past, with the farmer an entrepreneur, an inventive jack-of-all-trades, a rugged isolationist and individualist. When we revisit a rural area, as likely as not the man who meets us at the train will be wearing a suburban suit and driving a station wagon or an Imperial. He will take us to meet his wife, who cannot possibly fill the role of Reuben's Rachel any longer, for the chances are she is dressed at least as fashionably as her city cousin. A tour of the farm reveals it to be a veritable laboratory of specialization, its fortunes interlocked with those other units both rural and urban in character. The bookkeeping will be complex, carried on in what resembles an office. The farmer's attitudes toward life fit none of the antique stereotypes of Farmer Jones. He gets his signals elsewhere than from the farm.

Political, economic, and ethical attitudes are usually shaped in rural America today by the same forces as in the cities. This is an evidence of the dialogic violation of the old boundaries through mass media of persuasion and advertising. The packaged image of the Good Life promoted on network television is almost entirely urban, yet it reaches into most farm homes daily. The minister and the community leaders are city folk, whose adaptation to the rural environment is usually somewhat artificial. Harry Ashmore in his "Epitaph for Dixie" records some of the changes that extend even into the "rural" South:

> My generation is the first to have its roots severed entirely by the sharp edge of change. Some of us still live on the land, of course, and make a living from it. But today's farmer has the manner and the accoutrements of the corporation executive. He spends as much time bending over a hot telephone as he does walking his fields, he is a constant commuter to the cities now only minutes away, and the old home place has been remodeled. . . . You can't go home again. . . . This is true because home no longer exists.[5]

If we follow our diagram toward the urban concentration we encounter next the small town. A recent book, Vidich and Bensman's *Small Town in Mass Society*,[6] convincingly describes the sweep of the changes in class, power, and religion in this kind of community. It is ambivalent in its attitude toward mass society (let us hope so!), but rural values are indeed on the defensive. Through the ubiquitous mass media of communication, through migration in and out of rural communities, through the economic nexus, the small town has imported culture from the mass society. Also, it has its occupational gatekeepers to the mass society among professionals, businessmen, rural industrial workers, and the "rational" as opposed to the traditional farmers. Political surrender to mass society is extensive and the sociopsychological cost of the surrender is exorbitant. Even legal puritanism is moving. As Brogan somewhere reminds us all, it "now finds its political driving force in urban Catholicism, not in rural Protestantism."

The next circle of panurbia presents the greatest difficulty to the reporter of today. We speak of life in the suburbs. But the suburban complex is not a place but a state of mind that reaches everywhere from inner city to outer farm. Suburbia has come under so much study partly because it has been the new goal of American movement and as such has been the most fertile field for the sociologist.

Suburbia is indeed the best place to be sitting today to view the wave of America's future. Here the promise of American life seems to be realized; here the New Americans congregate in observable numbers and modes. Thirty or forty years ago the place to be in for studies of this type was the industrial-residential areas of the great cities; today the fringe areas of sprawling suburbia offer an excellent vantage. The physical growth of suburbia, says *Fortune,* "is portentous even in a country accustomed to talking of growth in superlatives." In its study of the exploding metropolis the magazine stated that 3000 acres a day of greenland were being bulldozed under for the use of an urban sprawl called, for want of a better term, suburbia. The term no longer implies simply swank, the Main Line or Lake Forest or Westchester. It now includes even the lower middle class in the mass-produced towns like Lakewood, the Levittowns, and Park Forest.

These are the concentrations of people that have attracted social analysts in numbing number. The psychic effects of life in suburbia and its shattering of the illusions of the American Dream are now too familiar to warrant further documentation here. David Riesman has made much of the uniformity and conformity of suburban life, but he goes beyond this superficial analysis that contents most of his colleagues. He hit at the heart of the problem posed for religion in suburbia when he directed his study to the meaninglessness, the aimlessness, and the "pervasive low-keyed unpleasure" of the life of many of its citizens.

"New, new, new," are these people, "like no other people who had ever lived," according to the late John McPartland in his novel *No Down Payment*. But the most important aspect of this "newness" is often overlooked. Most of the studies of the *new* suburbia take as their subject *the new arrivals who bring their values with them*—a fact that shows the extent of the panurban complex and the urban monopoly. The sociologists converge on new housing areas, studying people who scarcely have their bags unpacked from their former places of residence, usually apartments in the heart of the city. They have not had time or opportunity to be bombarded by suburban-developed values. They have brought something with them.

This was the point of Anthony Winthrop, Jr.'s, "perfect squelch" review of John Keats' *The Crack in the Picture Window*. Winthrop asked whether a "bigger house in a better integrated neighborhood" would have improved the life of Keats' fictional couple, the Drones. Could it be that they would find life hell wherever they went? Winthrop concludes with another "text" for our meditation:

"Hell, after all, is portable."[7]

If hell is portable, so, contend the churches, is heaven. With an impressive zeal they have converged with packaged heaven on the suburbs. This zeal combines creative vision for the future with a retreat from past failures in the city and an almost pathetic hope for better successes. Except when it involves abandonment of other fronts, there should be no occasion for the widespread criticism of the churches' mission to the suburbs *if it is really a mission*. The place where the American future is being shaped—whether or not we like the prospect—seems an excellent place for churches to be active. In this connection it is curious to see how defensive and apologetic many suburban church workers become when they are in mixed (i.e., nonsuburban) pastoral company. Their critics often suggest that a suburban ministry is a betrayal. The suburbanites who are served are sinners—*the* sinners, today, because of their selfishness and lack of Christian vision. The implied *non sequitur* in the historic sense of Christian mission is: therefore have nothing to do with them. This approach lacks compassion as it lacks logic.

Yet the criticism does come with reasonable warrant because the mission to the suburbs has often failed to be a mission. American churches are indeed vulnerable for their adaptation to, and identification with, the nonreligious values of suburbia which, after they acquire a thin veneer of religious terminology, are made to look

Christian. To repeat the grossest understatement of this book: the Christian mission exists to save people from something for something. The suburban church tends to baptize existing values and to sanction existing complacency. According to standard criticisms, suburbanites like their gospel—unlike their martinis—diluted, and the peddlers of dilution are legion. A two-dollar tour around the suburbs is sufficient for anyone out to gather documentation for such charges. At this point we can profit from two typical witnesses.

Gibson Winter wrote of a church in suburban captivity:

> Suburbia looms as a controlling factor in American church life. . . . We have all connived, albeit unwillingly, at selling the churches into a suburban captivity. The captivity of the church is a national tragedy of the first order, for it occurs at a time when America's position of world leadership requires a prophetic church at home. Suburban leadership is the antithesis of the prophetic note in the gospel. No one welcomes this prophetic note; to take it seriously is to make the initial, radical break with the suburban mind *in which all of us share.* [Italics mine: "hell, after all, is portable."][8]

There are positive values in suburban life. The activism of the do-it-yourself cult can be turned to religious ends. Family life is naturally strong and can become church-centered. But the suburb also poses "a threat to the church's witness to Christ's lordship"; it "has introduced its concept of success into the very center of church life." Advancement, monetary and numerical extension of power—these are the measures. " 'Salvation' and 'redemption' are disturbing to suburbia . . . the biblical faith is rarely met with [there]." Again: "The church's insulation from the world was not created by suburbia; it has simply found its consummation there. In a sense, suburbia expresses most fully the secularization of life which has accompanied industrialism. It represents the final step in the secularization of the church." Hence it deserves central attention in a study of the effects of panurbia.

Stanley Rowland, Jr., said substantially the same thing in the *Nation* for July 28, 1956. Nowhere is the church more popular or better off than in suburbia. Some clergymen crow with delight, but "many are shaking their heads gloomily," for "the suburban church worries the living daylights out of them." The Protestants in suburbia are insecure because another of their exclusive domains is tumbling; the Roman Catholic and Jewish movement to the suburbs is, after all, something relatively new. Cultural and religious identification in the Herbergian sense applies in all religious groups. "Churches and synagogues generally are affected by the suburban mentality, but Protestant leaders are the ones most vocally worried" over cultural identification on a wide, superficial, and generally unacknowledged level. The Holy Ghost, says Rowland, "had better stay ghostly and the preacher platitudinous," for sermons must console, comfort, inspire to pleasant living—but not challenge the suburbanite with the rude realities of today's revolutionary world. Tension between religion and society tends to disappear: "When organized religion is completely accepted by the mass as no more than a pleasing and fashionable facet of culture, then it falls prey to the mass-produced platitude."

Since, if we are right, suburbia is more a state of mind than a location, religious leaders dealing with "suburbanites" on farms or in cities should be worrying too. Here again the values crisscross as a result of the packaging of this way of life through mass media of communication. The bitterness often shown suburbia and the suburban ministry is perhaps an unconscious reflection of frustration over the perversion of the American Dream when we see it realized secularly. Critics of suburbia, having gazed at tree-lined streets and bright lamps in picture windows, find themselves entertaining the notion that this could be the Heavenly City surrounding the earthly city. But as they learn of the frustrations, anxieties, neuroses, and meaningless existences lived beyond the welcome mats of suburban homes, they too fall victim to disillusion. A friend of mine who is pastor to a minority ethnic group in the inner city was jarred to have it pointed out to him that the kind of life he was describing as a "fair break" for this own people would be simply a transplantation of the middle class suburban pattern he was in the habit of decrying.

At the same time the defenders of the suburban ministry often advance superficial arguments which fall short of their mark. Seldom do these spokesmen recognize the walls of insulation that suburbia has built around itself as a protection from a vision of the world's greater needs. At best the ministry they describe succeeds in infusing suburban life with a Christian approach to the wisdom of the ordinary. At worst it denominates as Christian what can be merely selfish motivations—concern for "the children," "my family," et cetera.

A typical defense was that of George S. Odiorne in *Presbyterian Life* (July 6, 1957). Odiorne pointed to these external dimensions: activities are not overextended, family orientation is healthy, all social strata are represented, groupness is a good thing, et cetera. It would be difficult to document his assertion that "the tendency to conformity which characterizes suburbia is, hearteningly, one which has as its model the proper mixture of doctrinal emphasis upon the Bible, the Lordship of Christ, witness in life and word." Most of the suburban churches that have been featured as models in our journals are notably short on theology, notably long on adaptation to alien values. It is time someone began to note the exceptions.

Suburban Protestantism operates under the same handicap that rural Protestantism did: it sees its own domain slipping away. Urban civilization is not Protestant, but suburban civilization once was. Perhaps as the sprawls around the city welcome a larger non-Gentile and non-Protestant population a purifying process will take place.

Such a process has been going on in the inner cities, the final zone that deserves concentrated study. The imploding metropolis with its decay, its ethnic changes, the rootlessness of its citizenry, has meant upheaval for evangelical Christian witness. But the trauma of these disturbances was felt some time ago—by the turn of the century or soon after—and the effects of urbanization have been repeatedly documented by historians. This no longer belongs to the new shape of American religion.

Protestantism had been nurtured on the soil and was never prepared to cope with the pavement. The very success of American Protestantism in evangelizing the earlier America limited it as it faced a later day. Protestantism is most threatened in present-day dislocation in cities because of its bad record and its still-obscured vision. In the most recent projection of the Federal Bureau of the Census, Protestants are estimated at 49.1 per cent in urban areas of more than 250,000 population, with Roman Catholics at 37.8 and Jews at 7.7. But in the dying rural areas Protestants num-

ber 83.2 per cent and Catholics 11.9 per cent. A table from a
church distribution study is informative.

	Metropolitan U.S.	Non-Metropolitan U.S.
1950 Population	57%	43%
Protestants	46%	54%
Roman Catholics	75%	25%
Protestant Churches	29%	71%

No one has measured nor knows how to measure the more significant secularization within and beyond these religious communities.
A fourteen-denomination study of new church development made
by the National Council of Churches suggests the sense of direction
now prevailing. Of new churches built in the ten years covered by
the survey, 19 per cent were urban, 17½ per cent rural, 63½ per
cent suburban.

Protestant Christianity is no doubt holding its own in town and
country and reaping a harvest in the suburbs. Since its greatest insecurity is in the city, we might take it as a cheering sign that by
far the greatest attention is now being given the mission to the
cities. As yet this interest is largely restricted to the urban church
workshops, the convocations on inner city work, the seminary
laboratories on metropolitan life, and the bureaus and institutes
of denominations and interdenominational agencies. If realization
of the true status of the churches in the cities could all of a sudden
be forced upon men and women who claim to have their faith's
interest at heart, their reaction would probably be either despair or
panic. But bit by bit the constructive realization of work to be
done and ways to do it is growing. It does not take long to assemble
an impressive file of groundwork already done for a new attack on,
and understanding of, urban church work, gathered from many
sources. A beginning has been made.

But of all Protestantism's thrusts, this is the one that has been
and still is doomed to greatest frustration. Truman B. Douglass
reminded the City Church Convocation of the United Church of
Christ in January 1958 of a line in a study document, a review of
mission over a century, prepared for the meeting of the World
Council of Churches at Amsterdam in 1948. It is a profound sentence, and a shattering one for those who have been complacent
about panurban America:

"There are three great areas of our world which the churches have not really penetrated. They are: Hinduism, Islam, and the culture of modern cities."

The culture of modern cities is spreading over America and is near universalization. A new concept is developing to sum up this fact: Interurbia. The term refers to the great interlocking urban areas that are taking over the map of America. One such area is the 600-mile city from Maine to Virginia through Boston, New York, Philadelphia, Baltimore, and Washington, which is broken only twice, once for two miles and once for seventeen, by non-metropolitan areas. The steel belt in Pennsylvania and Ohio is becoming another interurban area; so are Lake Michigan's industrial riviera and California's Los Angeles-San Diego complex. Mobility and growth will enlarge these and create others.

There is no place to hide.

If there were, the boundary-violation which is the result of mass media and mass culture would find the hermit. Radio, television, cinema, magazines, newspapers, and paperback books make high culture and low accessible to all. They help create the value patterns from which churches have scant opportunity to redeem men. These media are thoroughly secularized, even though they participate in the revival of religious interest and join in the current religious vogue. Yet in the very nature of things they must in fairness to all devote themselves first of all to religion-in-general or the religion of democracy. If occasionally they devote themselves to the individual faiths they do so cautiously and almost with a sense of guilt. When particular faiths are favored Roman Catholicism comes off best, partly because the richness of its symbolism renders it more congenial to the dramatic arts than its competitors for America's heart.

As the spokesmen of the popular revival itself are quick to point out, if one subtracts the expected article on a religious subject from a mass-circulation magazine, or the weekly network bout with religious issues from the rest of the television or radio calendar: would one be able to tell from the subject matter of what is left that religion—or specifically evangelical Christianity—in any real sense informs or once did inform our national culture?

When these media are put at the disposal of the churches the result is frequently embarrassing. Usually a pious overlay of secular values is presented as religion. As Liston Pope remarked: "An impressive number of programs under religious auspices appear on radio and television listings, but are there any religious programs?" Either "third force" Christianity utters its incantations further to alienate the alienated; or else, with few exceptions, public relational techniques are employed. God is packaged, man is depersonalized, the American Way of Life is proffered. Malcolm Boyd, who has made extensive studies of religion and the mass media, summarizes the state of affairs: The whole gamut of mass media tends toward religiosity amidst a climate marked by a combination of religious motivation and financial-power motivation. Judgment or grace is as hard to find as in the suburban dilution.

This then is panurbia, a physical change and a psychic invasion. Here is a pattern of values that Christianity and particularly Protestantism have not yet validly encountered. In the institutes on urban life anxieties are expressed, insecurities revealed, projects unveiled, progress reports made. Secular leaders in urban life and the field of mass media are accorded a hearty welcome. Representatives of suburban values repeatedly feel the sting of criticism. Theologians here and there reintroduce a prophetic note as counterpoint to the dirges for the dying faith in techniques as the answer. Couple this with selflessness, pan-Protestant sacrifices, co-operation—and a wedge for the Holy Spirit—and we may paraphrase the text for this sermon: "Well, urban civilization is not Protestant —*yet*." And the churches may yet make a beginning at penetrating the "culture of modern cities."

Six

Signposts to Theological Resources

I T IS clear that in describing the new shape of American religion I have been "taking sides." As historian, as journalist, as minister, as professing Christian I have exposed my presuppositions at many places. To admit less would be disingenuous. Few people are permitted the luxury of neutrality professed by Samuel Beckett:

I take no sides. I am interested in the shape of ideas. There is a wonderful sentence in Augustine: "Do not despair; one of the thieves was saved. Do not presume; one of the thieves was damned." That sentence has a wonderful shape. It is the shape that matters.

Ideas, in their various shapes, have consequences. We must now suggest some of the consequences open to one who might accept in broad outline the shape of American religion as described in the preceding chapters. It is always happier for programmers to work within the context of existing possibilities than to dream of a world that neither was nor can be.

The existing possibilities in religionized, post-Protestant America are different from those of the past—which does not mean that they are better or worse. Protestant Christianity has lived in many different settings and times. Prosperous America may provide a trap for it but it can also provide opportunities. In any case, this is a good time to be alive. Whatever criticism I have made in this book has been directed not at the fates nor at chance and change, but at an America that is known and loved and deserving of criticism, and at Protestant Christianity for its failure to live up to its own potential. What is required is that we evangelical Christians set out to be what we are defined to be.

The resources for dealing with the new religious constellation are at hand, latent in theology and in institutions and in men. In their resuscitation and renewal there is hope. For this task I should like to take as a text a word from a strange source, Pope Pius XI: "Let us thank God that He makes us live among the present problems. . . . It is no longer permitted to anyone to be mediocre." Since all our work comes under this judgment—including this present effort—it seems that the critical function within the churches must be kept alive.

Christians must be alert particularly in times of revival of interest in religion. During these years the "infidel," the legendary despiser of religion (cultured or not), has been relatively silent. Either he has "gotten religion" himself, or he just has not considered religion important enough to despise publicly, or most likely, he has found it unwise to deprecate a national religion which is so secure in its new setting that to criticize it would be construed as lack of patriotism or as giving aid and comfort to the enemy. At any rate, in his absence Protestantism has had to re-flex its atrophied critical apparatus.

When it did so there were those who forgot to what an extent this prophetic impulse is itself a part of Biblical and Protestant witness. To take one example: in the past the revivalist who tended to excess and paraded before the American public under the banner of Protestantism met his foil among the "lewd fellows of the baser sort" outside the church; the scoffers and the judges were there. Billy Sunday and William Jennings Bryan (who was also a revivalist in the first analysis) encountered their H. L. Menckens and Clarence Darrows. But when revivalism crested in the later 1950s the task of criticism fell upon churchmen. Christians who were informed in matters of religion and health were called upon to question Oral Roberts and the Tent-and-TV healers. Others who were concerned with the total Christian impact questioned the one-sidedness of Billy Graham's evangelizing. More often, they took issue with Protestants who were content to put their evangelistic eggs in one basket at the time of the Graham crusades. Instead of welcoming criticism for the benefit it might bring to the larger cause, many

Graham partisans wanted to write the critics out of Christianity. Such exclusivism is in no sense constructive. "There are a variety of gifts, but the same Spirit. . . ."

Having criticized, where do we go from here? It seems that we shall now have to "put up or shut up." But before we tackle the constructive task ahead, a brief backward glance is in order.

From the days when reformed Christians came to America "to practice the positive part of church reformation, and propagate the gospel" (Francis Higginson) to the present, Protestantism has carried on an exciting dialogue with its environment. The characteristic result we have described as *erosion*. Constant friction rubbed rough edges away. Protestant particularity and the offense of its witness tended to be worn smooth; uncongenial aspects in the American environment were absorbed. Church (or churches) and world made their peace. Religion was Americanized and America was religionized, and both were accepted complacently.

The revival of interest in religion in the 1950s once again made religion an aspect of culture worthy of intensive analysis. And in this exposed view it became clear that religionized America was not—at least not yet—a paradise. Men and women shared the Eden of the American Dream; but this fulfillment often left them frustrated. Seldom did the Christian faith seem to live up to its promise to judge or to save their world. The chief end of man (most of these people would have said) is or ought to be to give glory to God and to enjoy Him forever; but the God who was the product of America's climate of religion-in-general was neither worthy of glory nor capable of being "enjoyed." He was useful and used in a limited way; but a God fashioned by a nation is free neither to judge nor to save it. Man and God meet in sacred community: in denomination and seminary and family and parish; but so often this sacred community seemed merely to offer the values of its secular counterparts with a pious overlay that made everyone "feel real good" without giving them meaning.

Man. God. Community. I shall discuss three theological wells of resource for dealing with these in today's America. To begin the reconstructive task by pointing to theology implies that we may encounter there a not merely formal but substantial help in the complex problems of the day. Providentially or fortunately the central preoccupations of our century's theological renascence are germane to these three themes. The theological recovery is often seen as European in its origin, Continental in its "feel," and alien in its American ivory-towered transplants. Yet its central thrust can be brought to bear on these most "practical" American concerns. Theology and activism still stand each other off in an unnecessary impasse. Often we do not recognize our potential best friends.

It seems safe to say that the classic Christian doctrines which have most frequently occupied or obsessed theological discussants in the past quarter-century or so are the doctrine of man, the doctrine of God, and the doctrine of the Church—that is to say, anthropology, Christology, and ecclesiology. The three appear simultaneously and develop *pari passu*. Disillusion with the portrait of man painted in the era of belief in progress brought re-examination of the Biblical view of man and the insights of Christian history. Dissatisfaction with the limitations of the liberal portrait of God brought new urgency to the quest for Him in His condescension in Jesus Christ. Recognition of the necessity of "life together" in the modern world brought meaning to the life and teaching of the Christian Church. Let us take each of these in order.

The social analysts of the 1950s described a new kind of man emerging in our time. Their criticisms were virtually unanimous and were accepted as if from an oracle. The man of today, bewildered by the loss of true community, did not know who he was and where he was going. Economic and political forces in society, along with population growth, made it necessary for him to live closer to his neighbors. In this proximity he tried to find a new community and to draw his own from its values. He "conformed" to alien norms, became patternized and interchangeable. Authentic personhood began to disappear. Active though men may be, their apathy regarding many basic questions produced a curious and paradoxical passiveness in most. They lived under various pressures. Many turned to the churches for escape.

What was wrong with this picture was not that it fell short in its description of the externals of this new life or of the psychic damage external change brought. What was wrong, it seems to me, was that the analysts by and large asked wrong or partial questions and derived wrong or partial answers from them. They refused to counsel men to conform—as society itself implicitly did—because they knew that conformity violates personhood. So most of them urged men to rebel into various forms of individualism. Yet few people could break out of the circle. There were too few frontiers or islands or ten-acre plots of soil remaining for escape.

When we looked to see what "ideal man" lay behind the assumptions and questions of secular social analysis we found a fairly consistent image of what man was or might have been or ought to be, an image called independent, individualist, or autonomous man. Despite some qualifications, the man of the "Enlightenment" still formed the background for much of the questioning and counsel. This "Enlightenment" man is also behind much of the Protestant compulsion to create a new individualism, but here the portrayal is less refined than in the writings of the higher humanists. In crass outline the Christian individualists—be their concern directed toward a Christian economics or politics or church polity—have borrowed their man from the enlightened of this world.

Is it necessary to tie the hopes for the Christian Gospel to a view of man that was wrapped up in the eighteenth century and lasted through the nineteenth? Is it not a fact that Christianity has existed and even thrived in the presence of many successive portraits of man? Radical individualism appeared in the sequence for only a fleeting moment in the long perspective of history. To recover the larger view the Biblical witness is of great help.

This is the first of the three coincidences referred to above. Here theological recovery comes to confluence with a situation of human need. If we can recover the Biblical picture of man, perhaps we shall find ourselves less shaken by contemporary assaults on individualism. There is no reason for the churches' becoming confused into fighting a battle for a portrait of man they never needed. By this I do not mean that the Bible can be read as a codebook for answers or a road map for details. Its pictures of community differ from ours as do its pictures of men. But the relations of man to men in community and of man to God in community as revealed in that long span of history have been shown to have a curious relevance in our own time. Witness the fact that many of the more significant theologians of our decades have occupied themselves with just these concerns. Also, the existentialist contributions have largely been weighted on the side of the "doctrine of man," and the sciences of personality have claimed the interest of Christian scholars.

Even more important than these billboards calling to our attention the relevance of the Christian view of man have been the smaller signposts erected by Biblical theologians. (From my viewpoint all theology in the Christian tradition is "Biblical." By this use of the term, however, I refer to the work of those men who are first and foremost exegetes or interpreters of Scripture.) Biblical theology has come into its own as part of the reconstructive task that followed atomistic Biblical criticism. It received its impulse from the ecumenical movement where men from east, west, north, and south found that their only common language was the Biblical one. At any rate, in the grand sweep of all the "theologies of the Old Testament" we encounter attempts to recover the secret of authentic personhood in Biblical times.

Old Testament theological study has led so consistently to the question of man and God in community that almost any study in that field can serve as starting point for the attempt to bring together an ancient insight and a modern need. Ludwig Köhler's *Old Testament Theology,* recently translated, is a typical example. The evidence suggests, he says, that

in the Old Testament it is taken for granted that *man lives in a community,* comprehensive to a degree we can scarcely imagine. The community of the individual with the unit to which he is by nature assigned is unquestionable and is capable of settling a whole series of questions, theological questions included, which trouble us to-day. One can posit indeed that the theological concern of the Old Testament is not with the question of creating a community but with the question of the emergence within the community of individuals with personal value and personal responsibility.[1]

Köhler summarizes along five lines. Man in the Old Testament finds his life bound up with the lives of others. The community is of first importance. With the passing of time the individual becomes somewhat independent of this bond; equilibrium of some sort or other comes to play. It is God who calls some men out of the bond to charismatic existence: in other words, there is room for particular roles of particular importance. The purpose of the chosen or charismatic existence is not mystical relish of God's presence but rather the service of God for the saving of His people. Finally, the process is open-ended toward the future which will reveal an order in which all men prophesy. Köhler illustrates dramatically the part worship and the cultus, particularly the offering, played at each stage of this development. Throughout the Old Testament the concern is with "the People of God" and not with the persons of God. Yet strangely—or is it so strange?—the record of the People of God contains a sequence of pictures of persons as vital and moving as narrative art has ever painted. The Old Testament authors were capable of lifting people out of community and anonymity (common people as well as seers) and showing most memorably in what ways they were persons, were individuals.

At the very least the fact that the Old Testament community was made up of *persons* should mitigate Christians' feelings of insecurity in the face of the collective life. The question we face today (as Karl Barth recently pointed up) is not individual *versus* collective but: What kind of individual man and what kind of collective life shall there be? Not that we should yearn after Old Testament community patterns. These are impossible in our world. Men in those times were nomadic but they wandered always with the same group, their clan or tribe. We tear up our own roots and must seek new community "as seeds upon the wind." This individual mobility creates new difficulties and new compulsions. But again it does not contradict the idea that authentic personhood can be developed by and in community, even though some of our social analysts have been trying to tell us that man is an island, apart.

In the Christian witness the picture of man in community is brought further into focus under a new covenant—the "man in Christ" sharing the common life in the Body of Christ. Ecclesiology and anthropology have been fused in the study of the New Testament description of the *koinonia,* the shared life. Here the horizontal relations of man to men are characterized by participation in the divine life which is a gift from Christ (a vertical relationship). Here there grows a partnership of loving service and unity which draws its strength from the remembrance of Jesus Christ and the contemporaneity of his gifts.

Recovery of this conception out of which true individuality also

emerges has attracted many Biblical scholars and has exercised an
almost fatal fascination over today's practical churchmen. Many
have seized on this shared life as a gimmick, a device or trick
which, baptized with theological sanction, can be used to use
people. Almost any type of religious program can be promoted
under this banner and almost any type of human problem comes
under its promise. Here a caution might be in order. As one theological wordbook on my shelves has it (and this was written before
McCall's magazine began to monopolize the word), "Characteristic of the Church was a *togetherness* [sic!] far deeper than any
mere camaraderie."[2]

Misuse of this concept of New Testament togetherness came
under scrutiny in a fine review of Whyte's *The Organization Man*
by William H. Kirkland. After summarizing Whyte's thesis Kirkland pointed to a danger in the religious community, and did it
so well that I take the liberty of quoting him at some length. (I
wish I had said it.)[3]

We had better confess that this new character type and the ethic
emerging with it will be tricky and troublesome to criticize from the
standpoint of our Christian faith. For years now we in the Christian
church have been sounding the note of "community" ("participation,"
"togetherness," "belongingness," etc.)—so much so that a kind of
mystique has been created around the concept. Our motive was laudable enough. We were trying to meet the "urgent needs of modern
man" and to drown out the echo of the clarion call of "rugged individualism" that rang for so long on the American scene. But perhaps
we have now grown so sensitive to the dangers of bold and boastful
individualism that we have dropped our guard against the equally
dangerous advances of excessive groupism and togetherness, in which
the inevitable aloneness of man in his radical freedom and personal
responsibility is slowly absorbed and dissolved.

Hence we may hesitate to engage this new group interpretation of
life in frontal and flank encounter, for fear lest, in the name of
Christianity, we play into the hands of those unreconstructed thinkers
who have never qualified their contention that individualism is the essence not only of capitalism but also of the Christian faith. One can
imagine their reading these recent studies with great delight and saying: "We told you so! Look what social welfare, social action and
social Christianity have led to. We were right all along!"

Yet whatever the risk we must resist the tyranny in disguise which
this group-harmony ethic and group-directed character type represent.
This new emphasis on the group is not to be mistaken for a genuine
concern for the whole human community. It is not the same thing as
being *other-concerned,* or neighbor-*responsive,* as the Christian ethic

in its horizontal dimension must always be. It is a spurious concern if it results in abdication of personal freedom and a progressive dwindling of the self as an authentic center of decision and action. The individual person is in danger of so blending into the group that his thought and action becomes but a reflection or echo of the group—all this going on, perhaps, in the name of "community."

. . . From the Christian perspective, the obliteration of selfhood is the consequence. Man can be betrayed by trying to play God and by yielding up his freedom to a great collectivism. But he can also, and unwittingly, be betrayed by his psychological craving for approval from his peers. For the craving can don the moral dress of "brother-hood" and "fellowship."

The Christian faith, with its radical insistence, its always double emphasis—on *both* human freedom *and* true community, on both the "varieties of gifts" and the "unity of the Spirit"—this faith must alert us in this period in our culture to the insidious danger of having our personal freedom clouded and corroded by the feverish desire for group acceptance.

In this brief review I have tried to point to the Biblical conception of man's emergence from anonymity within and then in some sort of equilibrium with community; to see this emergence enriched by *koinonia,* a Christian participation that goes beyond togetherness or camaraderie; to urge that we safeguard this interest from per-version and manipulation by those who would twist it into a churchly device that might rob people of real selfhood. The theo-logical resources for understanding man developed in Europe and America in the past have only now begun to be brought to bear on the current problematic context; there is hope in the development of the trend.

Mr. Kirkland's concern for "other-concernedness" or "neighbor-responsiveness" as checks against the perversion of Christian com-munity coincides with the second great theological preoccupation of our time, Christology. We may credit the ecumenical movement for much of the renewed interest in this central Christian question. The people of separated churches have learned that they can begin to find one another again not through programs and platforms and platitudes but "vertically," by finding one another first in God's activity in Jesus Christ. This Christological concern is now so much taken for granted that we are conscious of the newness of its recovery only when we have occasion to look up the periodical literature or publishers' listings of three decades ago. More than we remember, the American theological world at that time was expounding a theology of "the First Person of the Trinity." A doctrine of creation and providence, Lordship and Fatherhood, along with a free-wheeling approach to the Holy Spirit and an often sidelong though reverent glance at the gentle Master, Jesus—this seemed to exhaust the proclamation.

Christologically speaking, we are not yet living in the best of all worlds, but we may take courage from the direction of recent thought. After the demise of the "Jesus of history" school emphasis was again placed on traditional teachings: the Incarnation (particularly in Anglican theology), the Atonement (particularly in Lutheran theology), the relation of the divine and the human in Jesus Christ (particularly in Reformed theology). All these seem to turn on one hinge—the door to the Christian doctrine of God in Christ provided by Paul in Philippians 2:

> *Have this mind among yourselves, which you have in Christ Jesus,* who, though he was in *the form of God,* did not count equality with God a thing to be grasped, but emptied himself, *taking the form of a servant,* being born in the likeness of men.

I have italicized some passages to suggest the connection between humanity and Christ Jesus, who took the form of a servant.

Is not this a second throughway down which Christian thought might proceed? Traveling on such an avenue, we might bypass the barrier between "theology" and "activism." Here are further resources for rescuing religionized men from the somewhat meaningless church life of the latter-day religion-in-general climate. What was wrong with the conception of a packaged God was that He demanded nothing of man. The vision of the Cross seldom appeared as a judgment. God promised only what His salesmen offered. What was wrong with religionized man in the Christian context was that the patterns which molded society in general molded him too—despite his deeper commitment and larger perspective. He seemed passive and often uncreative because the only options presented to him were old-fashioned "do-it-yourself" counsels of individualism sanctioned on Christian grounds. He was under pressure to produce a rich life out of shallow soil. He seldom had the idea or the person for which he might give himself.

Meanwhile, theologians have been quietly going about their

business. They have suggested that "the form of a servant" best characterizes God's condescension in history and His identification with His creature. They have shown how He revealed Himself as an authentic human person in fear and anguish before death, who yet "became obedient unto death, even death on a cross." They have agreed that death did not exhaust the possibilities of Jesus Christ: "Therefore God has highly exalted him and bestowed on him the name which is above every name." And man, says Karl Barth, is the creature "made visible in the mirror of Jesus Christ." Professor Alexander Miller, in a book which takes its title from that phrase, urges that in face of this mirror "the death of the self is the beginning of selfhood."[4]

Whenever churchmen relaxed and luxuriated in the climate of revival of interest in religion they forgot this. When Christianity was tied only to promise and never to commitment the self could not give way to true selfhood. When positive material goods were the promised result of positive spiritual thinking the Christian community often was perverted into a selfish circle based on clubby camaraderie.

All this points less to a program than to an impulse. The shape of evangelical Christianity and its quality in human lives depends upon men's sharing the form of a servant. The churches and Christian people can give of themselves in more ways than we need document—and indeed many are so giving of themselves. Some are reining in, in their headlong dash for statistical success and financial security, a dash as often as not prompted more by material or competitive or personal ends than by genuine compulsion to share the Christian witness. They should be enjoined to give up some of their prestige and security by speaking out in judgment where they are and upon themselves. An example: the tragedy of racial tension in the South has provided many clergymen with a new opportunity to witness to the offense and healing of the Christian Good News. This time of trouble may help lead to a new time of triumph. There are exciting possibilities in sacrifice and even, in ways we cannot now envisage, in selflessness and vicarious suffering. These might give us a foretaste of glory of the kind now talked about but seldom experienced. A cutting edge would return to

Christian proclamation. True individuality could be the by-product for those who had the courage and the grace to "empty themselves" and take the servant form. We have all at times seen such "emptying of self" in lives of people we know, and it never loses its power to move us. There is still place for Christian "other-concernedness" and "neighbor-responsiveness."

Man and God meet in community. A third resource for dealing with the new shape of American religion comes out of theological research into ecclesiology. This is the century of the collective life and the organized life and the United Nations. This is the era that saw the rebirth and the maturation of the Christian ecumenical impulse.

This is the time in which the "doctrine of the church" has claimed the study of scholars in every continent. At the hazard of neglecting other vital insights from this research, we shall explore one concept which can provide much mileage on the American landscape. This is the idea of "the Remnant." Of Old Testament lineage, the Remnant is subject to much sectarian misinterpretation, but it deserves ecumenical exploration.

With the erosion of particularity and the blurring of the line between church and world, the "People of God" has come to be a relatively meaningless conception. Everyone "belongs" with minimal commitment at minimal expense. Success-minded congregations make it all too clear in their solicitation that admission to the church is by handshake with the smiling pastor. The church that opens its door so easily loses its potency to evoke authentic personhood out of community. Few are asked to take the form of a servant, but all are frequently asked to take a packet of envelopes for financial contributions. No one is religious because everyone is "religious."

In time this near-merger of the community of Christians with the religionized community was challenged. In the new United Church of Christ there was a call for "integrity of church membership." Theologians began to speak of the "Strangeness of the Church" or of the church as the "Besieged City." There is enduring point in the discussion which appeared over the name of church historian Winthrop Hudson a number of years ago, *The Great Tradition of the American Churches.*[5] Hudson was speaking not so much of religion in personal life as about religion in America. After arguing the validity of separating church and state he remarked concerning the " 'disturbing discrepancy' which now exists between the size of the churches and the influence which they exert in American life." He feared that Americans were not sufficiently heedful of their own historical experience or of the recent events in Europe, where churches had "been forced to decide whether they [were] to be Christ's church or the church of a national religion." He criticized a pamphlet issued by the Commission on Evangelism and Devotional Life of the Congregational Christian Churches for its counsel that Congregational churches should make much of their assets, one of which, the pamphlet said, was that they "fit the mood and standards" of a community. Discipline and evangelism, Hudson pointed out, break down when church and community become coextensive, and worship tended to become meaningless in the growing American pattern of low-standard church life. Indeed, Hudson went so far as to urge that the "exclusive church," properly understood, be recognized as having a new validity. Perhaps, he said, even "fencing" the Lord's Table and insisting on the renewal of the covenant prior to Communion should be restored. He quoted Reinhold Niebuhr:

> Whatever the weaknesses of the "sectarian" church, which has set the pattern of American church life, one should think that the prevailing secularism of modern culture might give the idea of an exclusive church new validity.

For the recovery of integrity of membership and clarity of witness the Remnant concept has validity. Remember: the moment the word is introduced it becomes subject to misinterpretation. One cannot point to the people of the Remnant. The Remnant is not a "nice little nucleus," something one "joins." It is not a club, a social elite, a snob group of holy men and women. It is not to be found in the congregation whose spirit was parodied in a sermon: "We are all here on earth to help others: what on earth the others are here for I don't know." "The world" would have a perfect right to look askance and be offended at the wrong kind of offense from a prideful "city set upon a hill." The man was correct in his surmise to his psychiatrist: "So the meek are going to inherit the earth? I'd like to see how meek they'll be when they do inherit it."

No, the Remnant is an impulse, a thrust; never, never is it a definable group. Cornelius Loew once said in a discussion of Luther, "Only those go to heaven who are willing not to go."[6] If he means what I think he means, he has described a qualification for being of the Remnant. Only the man who is really a person, only the man who is fully obedient and trustful toward the God who is really God, is free to act for his fellow men without first considering merit or reward or consequence. Which is to say that each Christian derives his impulse and his values from a "vertical" relationship to God, out of which his horizontal relations to his fellows grow.

Is this motif part of the proclamation and discipline of our churches? Each of us must ask this for himself. Each of us receive many clues, as I did when hearing a thoughtful journalist speak to a ministers' group. In the course of other worth-while remarks he reminded his hearers that he was the village president in a respectable community and also a member in good standing of the church in which he was speaking. He said that in his first two years of dealing with people in his capacity as leader, he had often found himself reflecting on the quality of churchly commitment. In his village there were a prestigiously successful community church and a sizable Roman Catholic church, along with the full complement of churches of other denominations. But he said, had someone been leaning over his shoulder during all these contacts with the citizenry, asking him to point out which were "church people" and which were not, he could not have done so. Nor could he identify any values in operation which might have been derived from the religious institutions of the community. This confusion was true even though he knew a majority of the people to be committed members of churches. He knew of not one instance where the quality or character of a life seemed better or even different because of its commitment. No minister rose to challenge the observation. We knew.

Such a society ought to be a challenge to the Remnant, the daring and radical People of God. They won't look happier or more sad than other people. They will not need to shed the badges and the garb of ordinary life. Remember the people's comment on Kierkegaard's true knight of faith:

> Good God! Is this really he? Why, he looks like an Inspector of Taxes! . . . He belongs wholly to the finite; and there is no townsman dressed in his Sunday best, who spends his Sunday afternoon in Friederiksberg, who treads the earth more firmly than he; he belongs altogether to the earth, no bourgeois more so. *In him you will find no trace of that exquisite exclusiveness which distinguishes the knight of the infinite*. He takes pleasure in all things, takes part in everything, and everything he does he does with the perseverance of earthly men whose souls hang fast to what they are doing. [Italics mine.][7]

The knights of faith will look like other people; but there will be a difference. To return to an earlier illustration: In a community that has been racially monolithic, the village president would be able to spot the mark of the Remnant. There is an "incident"; complication enters; selfishness and segregation and hate rear their obscene heads. No one stands up. Then, suddenly, some do stand up, and they are able to say why they do—on Christian grounds, beyond the compulsion of law. These people give some substance to their commitment. Sharing the form of a servant, they too endure the Cross and despise the shame. Then a brick is thrown through a church window; a despicable label is painted on the door of a house of God; membership for the moment declines. But, for a glorious moment, everyone knew and everyone knew why. Events like this *do* happen.

In exploring further the idea of the Remnant we must remember that we cannot simply borrow a Biblical conception and superimpose it without translation on our day and place. In the Old Testament the Remnant came into being in times of great disaster. We should hardly be ready as yet to characterize the new shape of American religion as in every sense disastrous. Further, the Remnant is righteous, but a contemporary and temporary creative minority impulse cannot pose or point to itself as righteous. Augustine is right: we must not presume. But life for the larger community goes on and is nurtured and enriched by the Remnant. The Old Testament Remnant was to dwindle and did dwindle; but the New Testament Remnant was to move from a center and to grow through the world. That is still its task.

What is to be preserved from the Remnant picture is its double-sidedness. *On the one hand there is a full human identification with every aspect of life in the larger community; thus communication endures. On the other hand there is a sense of separation; here is the place for integrity, for commitment and vocation.* The substance of present-day theology can here change the forms of religion.

So we come to consider the most prominent locus of these forms as they affect most Christians in America.

Seven

The Poise of the Parish

IN DISCUSSING the forms through which theological insights might shape American religious life, we shall be dealing in a positive way with institutions. For my own part, I must view "anti-institutionalism" as a cheap solution and emphatically disagree with its proponents. Too often the critics of contemporary religion join in massive assault on congregation, seminary, or denomination. New iconoclasts, they would shatter the forms that centuries have developed and that the good sense of Christian people has brought to maturity. Misapplying a theorem of Henri Bergson's these iconoclasts assume that religious ferment must always harden and crystallize in its second generation.

The historian and the reporter, however, must turn with some hope to institutions. And I for one believe that *we already possess the institutions we need to undertake the religious task set before America today*. This book is not an argument for novelty or patchwork devices. Still, the institutions of Christianity in America need constant scrutiny. They must be revised; they must grow; they need to be purged. Every one of them has two aspects. It can work toward further erosion of vital lines—to violate the Christian view of the essential nature of man, to obscure the Christian portrait of God, to pervert a Christian view of community. Or, with proper investment of courage and ideas, it can help clarify the tasks of a new day and be servant of the servants of God.

It is not through arbitrary choice that I shall concentrate on the local congregation.* The reasons should be obvious. No other form of church life shares directly in the lives of so many people. No university system, no chain of seminaries or publishing houses, holds the potential the parish system does. To most people the word "church" does not bring to mind the universal Church that would probably be pictured as an abstraction or a cloudy blob. Rather, the word evokes an image of "the Methodist Church" or "the Baptist Church," or perhaps the First Congregational Church in their home town, or the Prospect Community Church which they plan to attend some day.

Our empirical breed's distaste for the abstract or remote and love of the known, the near, and the tangible stands us in good stead here and brings us into some sort of coincidence with the viewpoint of Biblical religion. The church was never an idea, a Platonic community; it was "the People of God at Corinth," or the *ekklesia,* the called out and gathered flock at a specific time and place. Even where St. Paul could have used abstract terms he chose to employ an offensively visible metaphor: the church was the Body of Christ. It was the church of various cities and the church gathered in various houses. The parish clearly has honorable lineage.

It has its dangers too. The picture of the local church is so powerful that it tends to exhaust the definition of the church. Partisans of the parish are inclined to romanticize its possibilities. We shall have to keep in mind the plenitude of things the local congregation can *not* do. But we must begin with the parish because, as the late Pope Pius XII and most American Protestants would argue, it is the "front line." It is the cutting edge of the church against the world. Because it is a long edge it is seldom honed. Yet it must be sharp, ready for all eventualities. Moreover, the parish too must take upon itself the form of a servant. It must serve and suffer vicariously for its community and the world,

*The term "parish" on these pages often is a simple equation of "local congregation": A local ecclesiastical society or organization, usually not bounded by territorial limits, but composed of those persons who choose to unite under the charge of a particular clergyman or minister" (Webster's New International Dictionary). Where the classic territorial setting is implied in the use of the term "parish," the context will make this clear.

"always carrying in the body the death of Jesus, so that the life of Jesus may also be manifested in [its body]." When St. Paul, according to the book of Acts, was journeying to Damascus to persecute the church there, the voice of the Lord said, "Saul, why do you persecute *me?*"

With all this weight upon it the local congregation is in a tragic situation. It has come to symbolize the point where the unfortunate impasse between theology and activism is absolute. The myth of the necessity of this impasse finds its plausibility in the difficulty of theologians' ideas and in the busyness of the parish minister and his people. The myth is nourished by the pride of the two camps. Sometimes the intellectual community looks down its nose at the parish and seems to relish ideas to the degree that they are untranslatable. And the impatient parish minister often does his share to perpetuate the stalemate. Pointing to his personal charm and his statistical successes he may argue that he does not need theology to keep his machine rolling. There are other factors. A strand of inherited anti-intellectualism in our nation's religious life; our impatience with the difficult idea; the force of experiential religion with little substance to it—all conspire to heighten the difficulty.

It is entirely possible that if this stand-off lasts much longer, the recent theological recovery will have been to little avail and the American parish may prove to have gained its whole world and lost its own soul. The notion that religion is to be nurtured apart from ideas and should be beyond criticism is a modern heresy. The Christian tradition gives us no comfort here, no ground for hope that the church can long sustain itself on momentum, on programs and on techniques alone.

One of the special difficulties in generalizing about the parish is that the experience of each of us is relatively limited so far as vital contact with many congregations is concerned. Only recently has interest in the parish matured to the point where critical scholarship is undertaking to study it. Much of the past literature on the subject is either merely promotional or programmatic, or else it tends to be of the romantic survey type. Further, "American pastors seldom write about their work. They lack the time, or the inclination, or both."[1] And the social analysts have written from the outside and often without sympathy. Depth studies of the parish should be a crucial next step in American religious thought. The parish is poised to help us today. Abbé Michonneau has written of this advantage in a paragraph that can apply to the American scene. The parish is strategic, says the abbé,

firstly, because it is already existing. Whether it plays its role or not, *hic et nunc,* the parish is a fact. It is, by right, if not in reality, that tiny cell of Christianity, of the Incarnation. . . . Every community has its own. Not even the civil government is as well organized. . . . And that is not all, for a parish is equipped. It has its priests, and parish clergy have always been the mainstay of the church's force. They are, or can be, or should be in permanent contact with their people.[2]

All this is a complicated way of reinforcing a simple point: any discussion of the future of the churches in America must concentrate on the local parish. For the parish is well poised, both geographically and in the hearts of the people.

Despite this poise, the local congregation is operating under handicaps. It is under extreme pressure in its hour of prosperity. The pressures are not of the persecutory type; few martyrs are emerging. And besides the church has always managed somehow to survive the catacombs. But it has done less well in surviving *as the church* when fused with its environment into a culture-religion. Most of the compulsions which force themselves into the consciousness of American church people are results of a culture that expects ever more accommodation and adaptation.

Let me illustrate by offhand reference to five types of pressure that the reader will recognize. To the degree that the churches relieve themselves or are relieved of each or all of them, they will become free for the tasks of reconstruction. The first is pressure from the society which surrounds the local congregation. By now it is not necessary to enlarge upon what has been documented throughout this argument. We have been saying that society expects a comfortable adjustment by the church to alien norms, and that American churches have in the main been too ready to comply. We see this in the application of success standards and in the quest for status—the things that "the Gentiles seek." If the local congregation takes its signals from its environment it will not be able to extricate itself from the world of the "others" whom it exists to judge and to save. The church is given a large but safe place in every community. The minister is often regarded with respect but without great expectations. Cautious church architecture is pleasing to the advertisers; it is a sure-fire symbol to use as background in their advertisements of new automobiles, a perfect image to illustrate a Way of Life. Churches of this sort are a chunk of Americana which we cannot well do without. Children are often sent to Sunday school on the theory that their social and educational balance is not likely to be out of kilter by the religious instruction they get there. Churchgoing is a habit which will serve the community or make happier homes. Such are the churches that are used by their environment, or rather taken captive by it.

It would be in poor taste to blame the children of darkness or of twilight for the pressures put on the local congregation and let it go at that. The children of light too are capable of loading the local church with more freight than it can bear. It is through the organized life of a denomination that a second kind of pressure results. Whenever themes such as we have been discussing are presented to any ministers' group, the nearly unanimous complaint comes back: "We are not free to go about our business." Every local parish is expected to pull a certain weight for the denomination, whose program and progress are portrayed as the marks of the march of the Kingdom of God.

In the face of this pressure no clear alternatives present themselves. It is easy to say that one ought to obey God rather than men and that churchmen and -women are responsible to Him and not to budgets and bureaus. But this often charters irresponsibility and allows the self-styled rebel to write out his ticket for laziness or selfish isolation: he need only refuse to support projects of a scope larger than the local. The individual parish does not serve the larger cause symbolized by the work of interlocked and united congregations when it refuses to close ranks and join in common tasks. What can it do? In most Protestant denominations it can express itself to some avail before the projects are planned. And it can find ways of revealing its attitude to a given project even while co-operating in it.

Initiative here, however, must come from the sponsoring boards and bureaus. They need to be subjected to the same kind of criticism that every parish accepts. The report forms of most denominational boards of missions, evangelism, and stewardship are testimony to the strength of the statistical pressure. Some boards hand out report cards to record a mere statistical success which does not account for personal and spiritual factors. Denominational stewardship appeals, clothed in spiritual language, often degenerate into appeals to lesser motives when the going is rough. All this, of course, is familiar criticism and it can be overdone. Some of the devices just criticized have their modest place in helping determine goals and providing a slight psychological push. But the temptation remains to let them dominate. A willingness to step off the statistical treadmill for a moment, to lose status among the families of competing denominations, may be the better mark of stewardship and evangelism in the present moment.

A third type of pressure which is hardly worth discussion yet is almost universally felt is competition among local churches of various denominations. The local effects of the ecumenical impulse have dulled this competition somewhat, and a spirit of Christian brotherliness is a constant check upon it. But overchurching of new communities still proceeds apace. The world mission of the church is often forgotten in the scramble to build a tower higher than St. Babel's down the block. Again, documentation is less necessary than description. Many Protestant laymen or laywomen have experienced the necessity of sitting back and thinking through the reasons why a certain religious project is undertaken, only to find evidence that basic Christian motives were secondary to the old church tie.

A fourth type of pressure (by-product of the second type) is an equally common cause for complaint. To build up the institution, denominations have learned to play off parish against parish. This gambit is, of course, neither a recent development nor a Protestant monopoly. Use of it has simply been accelerated of late because of better communications within denominations. It occurs in all denominations. In his book *Protestant and Catholic*[3] Kenneth Underwood gives us an almost ribald account of the fund-raising competition of Catholic parishes in Holyoke, Massachusetts. Evidently competition there was most intense for the carnival dollar. The pastor of one church boasted to the author: "The annual Holy

Rosary Lawn Fete is the crowning achievement of a life of fund-raising for the love of God, which began with the best little beano game you ever saw on the lawn back of my first parish house." Holy Rosary is "New England's biggest and best fete," the pastor said. And besides, Holy Rosary is "the smallest parish in the diocese and has the biggest income in the city and perhaps in the diocese."

If we subtract the antic aspect we can discern here the kind of goading that is back of the conventional success stories of Protestant churches. He would be a sour soul indeed who wrote off entirely such human motivations as friendly competition. It is probably proper to boast that Beloved Disciple Church mauled the Prince of Peace basketball team, as the sportswriters put it, and to allow for a bit of semispiritual gamesmanship. But every religious group can provide ample evidence that the success stories of parishes are usually told with a different end in view: they absolutize the competitive principle at the expense of vital Christian motivations and means.

In this context we confront the twentieth-century counterparts in Protestantism of the ancient athletes of God or virtuosos of holiness; namely, ministers of "fastest-growing" churches. Observe the denominational conventions and a pattern will be clear. Somewhere along the line, one of the examples of achievement is paraded. He discusses the techniques that make possible the irrepressible thrusts toward holiness in his community. Every year it must be some new gimmick—the Bible Brunch or the Three-Dimensional Card-File System or the Hi-Fi Club, or perhaps some ancient counsel such as "a calling pastor makes a great church." The little dance usually goes on in front of an impressive backdrop of graphs, each of which surges relentlessly upward. No one mentions the faithful but failing churches.

Now the purposes behind these performances are laudable enough. The men who sponsor them and the men who enact them, if they are thoughtful for the moment, are capable of translating their entire effort most sincerely into one of conscientious evangelization of the world for Jesus Christ. The intention is that the success story shall inform and inspire the failures. But it does little to picture the real nature of evangelism and conversion.

Having chalked up all the possible favorable assets of a capable and winning parson, a dynamic parish program, and a wise adaptation of the newest techniques to ecclesiastical purposes, one gap remains. It must be closed by the Holy Spirit of God. Conversion remains a gift. Erik Routley has recently reminded us of this in a moving discussion, one of whose principal points seems to be that the Holy Spirit chooses to work with one person at a time and has not yet been informed of the mass successes of the latter-day programmatic Pentecosts.

> Conversion is not expertness. It is not knowledge. It is not skill in the pursuit of theology. It is not church work. It is not the sacred ministry. It is not a feeling of pleasure. It is not enthusiasm. It is the process by which a man is received into the presence of God, that as a child he may say, Abba, Father, and as a man may sit at the right hand of Jesus Christ in His glory, being baptized with the baptism with which He was baptized, being honoured through service, being exalted in humility, being in his life and example, in his bearing of contempt and in his patient and compassionate endurance of the central sorrow and despair of the world, a "ransom for many."[4]

All this may be a lofty statement in quasi-mythological language that may seem strangely out of context here. It is intended to be in context.

This passage of Routley's is preceded by some remarks on the "Success-Evangelism" which as a mode of life places undue pressure on parishes. This too is worthy of quotation:

> That in modern society which debases men and makes them as indecisive and dependent as children, that which lays them open to the assaults of dictators and of "Big Brother," must be not bowed to by the evangelists but sternly and penetratingly denounced as a corruption. The consequence of any attention to such a warning as this would be a realization that *conversion is a matter which will never be properly covered by statistics or describable by journalists; that is as may be.* But any political technique, or any evangelistic technique public or private, that treats men as children, assumes that they are and will remain irresponsible, and degrades them below the level of courage and decision is, however innocent its purveyors may be, corrupt to the heart. [Italics mine.]

It is precisely this corruption that takes place when the illusion is created that surface solutions and clever devices are capable of bringing about authentic conversions and vital church growth. Is not this simple reduction of a complicated spiritual experience to a promise related to external techniques tantamount to "treating men as children"? The illusion it creates has little to do with what we see forged in the souls of sensitive men and women through years of reflection and action.

In one other respect the admirable attempt fails. Designed to inform and inspire the failures, it generally succeeds in neither. The prodded men may admire or envy the successful techniques-man and may even introduce all his methods into their own provinces, to little avail. A good deal of needless vocational doubt grows out of this. As a reporter's conclusion that might provide some collegial therapy to others, clerics and laymen alike, I shall cite a canon which is of help in evaluating all these "successes": *Behind every story there is a "story."* Apart from the minor differences in gifts between men of God, the untold part of every story of inordinate success seems to come down to either of two alternatives. One, a parochial situation is promising and accounts for sudden growth; for example, when a congregation of a denomination that holds the loyalties of a certain ethnic or income-bracket group finds itself planted in a new community to which the group is attracted. Two, a congregation is tempted to "give the lady what she wants" and supplies a tailor-made Gospel, custom-fitted to the prejudices of men and women, offered at bargain prices in the absence of standards.

This leads to a parallel illustration. Several years ago *The Christian Century* printed a series of articles on "Great Churches of America." The churches were selected by the vote of subscribers to the magazine. In almost every case they equated "great" with "very large," and often for good reason: the smaller congregation has less opportunity of being known and of accomplishing notable or newsworthy achievements. So the "Great Churches" selection proceeded on proper ground rules and came up with proper results.

A couple of years later the magazine announced a second series, on Creative Churches of America. This time the questions of greatness and success were to be deliberately avoided. No one was polled. No one was solicited for suggestions except through personal editorial contact—in many cases, with metropolitan journalists or newspapermen. The editors were in quest of churches which were biting off problems larger than they could reasonably expect to manage and were ready to risk failure in the attempt. As printed, the series included a number of successes—churches which had finances or status behind their experiments. But the common complaint of readers was that most of the churches described could not possibly be very creative: they were not growing fast enough. Some ministers came forward to nominate churches more worthy of reportorial survey. They documented their nominations with impressive cresting graphs. The churches were usually their own. This *Christian Century* series had difficulty conveying meaning because our habits of mind hardly prompt us to look for creativity in a church that works in a tormented or dying or insecure community.

The result of this fourth kind of interparish competition can be a loss of sense of mission and purpose. When the reasons for the churches' existence are exhaustively defined by the terms "onward and upward" or "bigger and better," all other dimensions of religious life are lost from sight. The educative task, the training of the Remnant, and other proper functions of the church are relatively neglected. A church's clientele moves away, and the church follows them, abandoning its original area even when larger population concentration then opens up greater possibilities for it. The minister who is not content to have a parish "a mile wide and an inch deep" tends to experience a sense of meaninglessness or frustration.

None of this chapter is to be taken as a criticism of growth and the extension of the Church; that would be absurd. It simply asks the question of terms of growth and types of growth and times for allowance of decline. It is, despite the sharpness of its ring, a plea for charity to be shown the countless men and women unequipped to tell their story, if they have one, as they go about their quiet religious tasks. With this in mind we can take a passing glance at a fifth type of alien pressure superimposed on a congregation. Rather, this is "subimposed" for it comes *from within* while it draws its resource from the types of competition and foreign norm described in the above four categories.

Symbolic of this misapplication of business canons to religious life is the familiar instance of congregations which goad their ministers into calling on newcomers "so that we can meet the budget," or which refuse to respond to the appeal that they evangelize with the answer, "We don't need more members; the budget for next year is already oversubscribed." This is the element that expects its minister to turn himself into a pint-sized Peale or a grassroots Graham, reproducing in a fashion unnatural to him the gospels which have been shown to possess a mass appeal. It is not necessary to elaborate on this.

To remove these pressures a variety of strategies may be in place. A good sense of humor, a shrug of the shoulders, and the ability to grin and bear it may be excellent equipment. The grace to cooperate in necessary tasks and the wisdom to perceive when the institution is a surrogate for God may help men and women discriminate. Knowing what is to be taken very, very seriously but not *too* seriously is another acquirable ability. And when these alien standards take on oppressive and even demonic forms, an ancient word of advice is still in place: "This kind of thing can only be cast out by prayer."

We have placed so much emphasis on the poise of the parish that it is also necessary to add that partisans of the parish and sentimentalizers of the local congregation do them a disservice when they weight them with more than they can bear. It is as much to the point to know what the parish can *not* be expected to do as to help free it to do what it should. The parish cannot become the intellectual nerve center—not because laymen and laywomen are not up to the intellectual pitch required, but because they are vocationally equipped to be and to do something other than this theological conception implies. Indeed, that ideal may attract dilettantes who will do the theological talk more harm than good. It seems hardly necessary to warn lest parishes become too well informed; but in the ivory-tower criticism of congregations an intellectualistic ideal is often expressed for them. The congregation needs to be shaped theologically, but it is not the intellectual center: it is the arena where ideas are put to test, the place of translation or encounter.

Similarly, dreams that the aesthetic problems of current religious life will be solved on the parish level will probably remain dreams. Certainly a number of exceptional examples of church architecture in recent years might inspire one to see great possibilities there. A number of congregations have produced excellent displays of contemporary religious art. But this will also remain a minority effort, the point at which the aesthetic impulse tends to be thinned out and compromised. Again, in matters of social justice there seem to be few limits for individual congregational expression, but many tasks in this line call for united action and for awareness of the interwoven destinies of members of the Church throughout the world.

The parish must first learn what it must not allow to disturb it; it must learn what its limits are. There are limits, though most of us are surprised to discover how remote they are. The parish is poised for the problems of our day. What seems to many the last place to look for hope may become the first. In each parish there may be what God alone can identify with certainty, the Remnant that can move a world.

Eight

The Practice of the Parish

IN THE external sense each local congregation is poised to make a greater contribution than it has yet made to shaping American religion. We have now to look at its internal life and again deal with several options in broad generalities. As usual, we must be conscious of the exceptions, though not bound by them. Up to this point I have been suggesting: first, that some sort of preliminary line must be drawn between church and world if the Church is to regain an effectiveness that goes beyond mere success; second, that the Remnant concept can inform the essential task of the local parish; third, that the local church must relearn what it can achieve and what it cannot be expected to achieve. Several approaches to parish life are now current in American practice.

One approach might be termed multitudinism. A second, its opposite, is irresponsible reaction to multitudinism. A third is responsible lay vocation with pastoral direction. On the irresponsible reaction to the busy-busyness of modern congregational activity we shall have little comment. Cavalier dismissal of the more routine aspects of church life helps no one. There is no avoiding the fact that life—including the spiritual life—involves people in prose and routine. The riches of Christian vocation are not to be easily or creatively attained if some detail work is not shouldered by ministers and lay people alike.

134

But we must pay more attention to multitudinism—a barbaric word but a good one for our purpose. It is borrowed from a book by Martin Thornton (which will be analyzed later). It sums up an idea: the local church must somehow touch *the maximal number of people in the community through minimal means.* The reconciling circle must be drawn in a large sweep (this is a charitable translation), even if it is stretched toward meaninglessness. The widest possible range of parochial activities must be offered and the sense of mission is to be judged by the success of the activities. Multitudinism is a partial denial of the Remnant concept, as we shall see later. The most conscientious parish priests and ministers are tempted to fall victims to it, at the expense of nurture and even of vital pastoral activities: laymen can become so organized and their activities so routinized that the machinery of church life, smoothly oiled, takes the place of the deity in many a hierarchy of values. Spiritual energies are dissipated.

Multitudinism begins by asking what nature of activities and programs are expected of a typical congregation—expected by the membership, the competition, the organization, and the society which invests little but looks for much. An illustration of multitudinism is offered by a dynamic programmatic suggestion titled *Organized for Action.*[1] We shall use it not because it is either more or less diffuse than other blueprints of this sort but because it is quietly and inoffensively somewhere in the middle range. Indeed every clergyman welcomes a practical suggestion of this nature, for it helps men to organize more efficiently and to see some new possibilities. There is no virtue in disorganization. Suppose, though, that someone adopted this pattern. Beginning at the beginning with this blueprint, what would our good denominational man in the local church encounter? He would see his place in relation to the following officers in addition to the pastors and paid staff:

> The Church Council and Chairman
> The President
> The Vice-President
> The Secretary
> The Treasurer
> The Board of Elders
> The Mission Committee
> The Athletic Director

The Financial Secretary
The Stewardship Committee
The Finance Committee
The Board of Education
The Sunday School Superintendent
The Board of Trustees
The Head Usher
The Youth Counselor
The Bible Class Enlistment Chairman
The Sunday School Auxiliary
The Music Committee
The Telephone Canvass Captain
The Women Visitors' Captain
The "Physical" Talent Co-ordinator
The Photography Co-ordinator
The Elders' Subcommittee
The Stewardship Subcommittee
The Women's League President
The Vice-President
The Secretary
The League Program Committee
The Absentee Secretary
The Library Committee
The Altar Committee
The Kitchen Committee
The Membership-Visiting Committee
The Special Projects Committee
The Nursery Committee
The Committee for the Sick
The Card Committee
The Publicity Committee
The Bible Breakfast Committee
The Motor Pool Co-ordinator

Allowing for three people per committee (a minimum, we can be sure) without the Sunday School Auxiliary, it would take at least eighty people to get the machine off the ground. The plan is recommended entirely aside from considerations of the size of churches. But a healthy minority of American Protestant churches do not even have eighty responsible adult members. Merely to co-ordinate the co-ordinators or to expedite the expediters would be a full-time job. Yet few Protestant parishioners will fail to recognize here a portrait of their own congregations, give or take a few committees here or there.

Meanwhile, according to the blueprint, there are files to be kept and records to be made. This would be an unnerving business even if each kind of file were kept by a different person; and then who would know the whereabouts and condition and correlation of each? The suggested examples:

Worship Bulletins
Talent Card
Soul-Accounting Record
Congregational Membership List
Address and Phone List of Places of Work
Congregational Scrapbook
"Car File" on Membership
Pastor's Sunday School File
Sunday-by-Sunday Church Attendance Record
Prospect File
Sermons File
Discipline Call File
Service File
Visual-Aids File
Stewardship Performance
Sunday-by-Sunday Record

and, may we add, a file-file? This is not caricature; this is standard procedure from which it is difficult for any to escape. The devotional life must find its way in all this. There is also the matter of keeping publicity operative:

The Public Worship Service
Letters-Mail
Brochures
Posters
Bulletin Inserts
The Telephone
Yearbooks
Calling Programs
Monthly Activities Calendar

All in all, this program is as good as any other. In some translation or other most parishes could reproduce its format and actually save some time in recovery from their present disorganized and schizoid state.

It is this form of busyness that brought up the discussion of clerical psyches and ministerial breakdowns several years ago. One counsel then offered was to turn detail work over to laymen. This strategy slights lay vocation. Moreover, no one suggested what to do with the laymen's breakdowns or crack-ups in the multitudinist burgeoning of thin-spread activities.

The most profound counsel of the 1950s came from H. Richard

Niebuhr, largely as the result of his observation of an emerging trend in parochial affairs. The minister, Niebuhr argued, was beginning to find a new role in the modern world, a role that differs as indeed it must differ from past conceptions of priest, preacher, or evangelist. It is summed up in the term "pastoral direction." Combined with informed lay vocation, this seems indeed the only creative solution. After we see what "pastoral direction" means, exteriorly, we shall try to bring it together with a Remnant theology and a strategy that might counteract multitudinism.

As opposed to the irresponsible bohemian or the "big operator," the pastoral director recognizes that while he may be in part an executive it is the *church's* work he administers. "His first function is that of building or 'edifying' the church; he is concerned in everything that he does to bring into being a people of God who as a Church will serve the purpose of the Church in the local community and the world."[2] His main work is the care of a *church,* the administration of a community that is directed toward the whole purpose of the Church; namely, the increase among men of the love of God and neighbor. In the process the Church becomes the minister and the "minister" is its servant, directing it in its service.

Our society has tended to make the *pastoral* director a pastoral *director,* often at the expense of lay vocation. If a minister is to be a minister to the Church's servants, he may go about many of the multitudinist's tasks; but he will have a charter of freedom, an attitude toward the relative importance of his various efforts and an exhilarating detachment from the slavery they threaten. Here he needs a new lease on life theologically. Here is where the greatest amount of thought ought to be given to the questions: What is a parish? What is the responsibility of a congregation to itself and its community? What is it setting out to accomplish?

To take the long road around as the shortest way home, I should like at this point to carry on a conversation with a book, whose title suggests what is here being called for: *Pastoral Theology: a Reorientation.*[3] It is written by Martin Thornton, Priest of the Oratory of the Good Shepherd in England. Few books in this field are more disturbing. Sometimes it seems to offer a clue to parochial life on the American scene; at others it seems almost perverse in its counsel. Perhaps this is because our senses of direction are "only analogous; that is, they are partly the same and totally different."

The book has been regarded by some critics in the Anglican communion as an alarming document, a charter for laziness on the part of parish priests who do not enjoy being busy. At times it seems to counsel the absurd. It operates with such variant counsels in a theological world so different that for an American Protestant reader to use it is somewhat like banging his head against the wall because "it feels so good to stop." Yet almost every page still tantalizes with the prospect that in the analogous situation there might be an insight for our own. It is to this book that I owe the distinction between two approaches to the parish, multitudinism and the Remnant.

Thornton's intention is to resurrect "ascetical direction" in the parish as ours would be to recall "vocational meaning" among men who will take the form of a servant. His asceticism is a much too narrow conception for dealing with the images of man and community in America today. We need at least a four-dimensional recovery: in worship, teaching, discipline, and vocation. His community of intercessory prayer for the surrounding community may be rewarding from the viewpoint of piety and justifiable along his rather sophisticated theological line of reasoning. It will strike the American Protestant, however, as having little to say about the matters which make up the stuff of his own life. Nevertheless, in the context of the erosion of theological distinctiveness and of the meaningful line between church and world, Thornton's overstatement of a case may help us draw some lines in the American setting.

First, then, a brief summary of the whole argument. Thornton suggests that it is unrealistic to picture the mass of mankind at any particular moment or place as being profoundly religious. But Christianity is a universal religion, in no way destined to be shared only by an elite or elect few. In a glance at the New Testament Thornton shows that just as Jesus "saved the whole world" without moving more than a few miles from his home and by concentrating on twelve men, so can the committed and faithful in any parish save the parish by being what Jesus was: an agent of a vicarious action. As all mankind was organically "recapitulated" in Christ, so are the surrounding multitudes "recapitulated" in the parochial

Remnant which exists to serve them. The Remnant lives under the discipline of the Church, with worship in community and "coaching" in private prayer at the heart of its activity.

Through Rule, the overflow of spiritual power into the world is a necessary, unalterable, and fundamental part of the divine plan. Once assured of this we can forget about converts until they arrive; which in God's good time they must.

Thornton's picture is that of the first team which represents a school. Not all members of the school play on the team, yet the school wins or loses each game. Thousands of supporters say "we won" or "we lost." Somehow or other the Remnant is to be the "first team" to represent the parish before God. As a good first team it will be taking care of parochial morale, just as a winning athletic team inspires the whole school or community and creates in others the wish to aspire. "There is nothing so contagious as holiness, nothing more pervasive than Prayer. This is precisely what the traditional Church means by evangelism and what distinguishes it from recruitment." The parish minister's job then is not to be tracking down all the individual people of his parish and compelling them to come in, but to be coaching his Remnant. Thus he avoids the danger of being "either a nice kind encyclopedic seer, or a licensed busy-body." Such a minister (or priest, in Thornton's terminology) would find his sense of pastoral direction and vocation. He would have a professional job in the best sense and could channel his energies to improving that vocation and his qualifications for it instead of dissipating them in senseless directions and with smatterings of knowledge.

Reviewers of Thornton's book have pointed to the pitfalls of this scheme: the dangers of irresponsible pietism and the temptation of the Remnant to become a self-conscious elite. Again, Thornton allows more to intercessory prayer as an "evangelistic technique" than would most of us, and he plays down the vital contact between man and man which is a theme of this book and in which the Christian parish can play such a vital part.

But any minister who is getting tired of being something of a Paulinist on Sundays and largely a Pelagian the rest of the week will find this book stimulating. It might even give him the courage to relinquish dreams of solving his parochial problems by hiring either a psychiatrist or a public relations expert, and to venture into the realm of prayer, both for himself and for his people.

Translating scenes and settings and terms, it may be possible now to see how the assets of Thornton's approach outweigh the hazards of presenting what at first looks like foolishness to many.

The problem of religionized America was this: everyone was "religious" and so it was hard for anyone to be religious. That is, when a culture-religion sank root in our society, taking captive with it much of the impulse of Biblical religion, it became difficult to see the need for deeper commitment and larger service. Culture-religion is by its nature all-inclusive; it offers without demanding and satiates without inspiring. Against this background the Christian parish, if it is to have something to say to society and if it is to represent him who "came to seek and to save that which was lost," must somehow begin its work by expressing a sense of "the Difference." Where Thornton prescribes Rule or Prayer, can we not prescribe "the Difference" in worship, teaching, discipline, and vocation?

It is in nurturing, preserving, enlarging, and then utilizing "the Difference" that the Remnant-hypothesis comes into guarded but rightful use. Thornton makes clear again and again that the Remnant is not the same thing as "the nice little nucleus." We can go further, to suggest that the Remnant is not often where parochial leaders think it should be. Often the institutional leaders of a denomination or a local congregation, instead of being the vicarious servants, may be sitting on and stifling genuine religious impulses that find sustenance in what now look like the edges of the churches.

Examples: The architect who designs for the church of God new chapels that, in their modesty, simplicity, and honesty, express something of the rough edge of the face-off between man and God is less likely to be identified as part of the Remnant than is the favored denominationalist architect who designs grand and sanctioned churches on safe, stereotypical, and "lovely" lines. But the indirect witness of the former may ultimately do more to express "the Difference" than do the practitioners of the cut-flower Gothic and Suburban Dress Shoppe schools of religious architecture. The student asking the proper questions or the recent convert struggling to shape a language of response may for the moment be grasping at the mantle of Remnanthood more assuredly than the newly orthodox seminarian reiterating the comfortable verities. The husband who has conquered alcoholism and is winning a shrewish wife back to responsible partnership seems to be at the edges of a congregation. But he may be a more vital example of churchly discipline in action than the safer ninety-and-nine which need no repentance. And it takes no great perception to say that many plumbers, legislators, teachers, and housewives have caught more of the sense of "the Difference" in vocation than has many an ordinand.

So the Remnant is not something that one joins, or that one's minister points to, or that one adheres to by adopting Thornton's simpler prescription. *The Remnant is rather a goal. It is a becoming instead of a being in the Christian community. It is a hypothesis, a remembered rubric from Biblical times, reborn for a new day.* It is a principle for supporting the essential tasks of the Church and of Christian worship. It is never this or that permanently identifiable group of people.

Yet one must begin where one is. Parochial leaders must begin by developing the sense of "the Difference" among those who show signs of deeper commitment. Their energies will go into enlargement of this core, not so much through multitudinism, through minimal contact with the maximum number of people. Instead (may we remove a comma from the English translation of Ephesians, chapter four?), the essential parochial task becomes the utilization of God's gifts *"for the equipment of the saints for the work of ministry, for building up the body of Christ,* until we all attain to the unity of the faith and of the knowledge of the Son of God, to mature manhood, to the measure of the stature of the fullness of Christ; so that we may no longer be children, tossed to and fro and carried about with every wind of doctrine."

Now Thornton's most offensively ironic line (so characteristic of his expression) begins to make sense: "[Jesus] restricts nine-tenths of his ministry to twelve Hebrews because it is the only way to redeem all the Americans." The parish begins by momentarily and strategically restricting its ministry, not for the cultivation of an elite but "to redeem all the Americans," to offer more in a time of illusory redemption or of merely salving salvation. This translation of Thornton into Americanese might be disturbing to him; it is the kind of hazard all men with good ideas set down in print expose themselves to.

The poise and importance of the parish here come into play again. The church has not only local significance but also national consequence: It has something to say in the "new shape of American religion." This can be shown in the obviously empirical sense. If the parish best illustrates what is wrong it should also serve as the best instance for seeking progress—a notion that may also have excellent theological rootage. Thus Thornton:

> The environment with which we can become in contemplative harmony, in which we can be lovingly "at home," can be expanded still further. We can truly be said to love our village or town or county or country—even the universe at large, which by the principle of recapitulation or microcosm becomes much the same thing. "God so loved the *world*"—yet the Son of God so loved by a microcosmic love for a few square miles of Palestine. All that concerns us, in following him, in being his Body in place as his Body was, and remained, in place, is contemplative harmony with, union with, love for, that environmental organism which we have called a parish.

There are senses in which this is a Christian translation of some secular counsel given by J. Robert Oppenheimer at the anniversary of Columbia University some years ago:

> We know too much for one man to know much; we live too variously to live as one. . . . Our knowledge separates as well as it unites; our orders disintegrate as well as bind; our art brings us together and sets us apart. Diversity, complexity, richness overwhelm the man of today. Superficiality and fatigue become the temptations of those perpetually and precariously balanced between the infinitely open and the intimate. [In such a time,] Each . . . will have to cling to what is close to him, to what he knows, to what he can do, to his friends and his tradition and his love, lest he be dissolved in a universal confusion and know nothing and love nothing.[4]

It is at the same time a world in which none of us can find sanction for any ignorance, any insensitivity, any indifference.

> This cannot be an easy life. We shall have a rugged time of it to keep our minds open and to keep them deep, to keep our sense of beauty and our ability to make it, and our occasional ability to see it, in places remote and strange and unfamiliar; we shall have a rugged time of it, all of us, in keeping these gardens in our villages, in keeping open the manifold, intricate, casual paths, to keep these flourishing

in a great open windy world; but this is, as I see it, the condition of man; and in this condition we can help, because we can love one another.

Here a high humanism and a broad theology come into confluence. Obviously, this strategy is not permanent nor does it solve all problems. In the light of a larger world vision it is too modest an approach. Perhaps it too much rolls with the punch of history, implying the tragic sense of life and counseling the wisdom of the ordinary. But it is not intended to be exhaustive, and it makes possible a beginning at solution of some problems. People who are free to lead in this strategy are free to unite with those who can bring a light for the larger vision. Beginning somewhere is better than acquiescing in a sense of futility.

If these ideas are to have worth in the local congregation, it remains to be asked, How will such a parish look and what will it do? To become programmatic at this point, to introduce plans which can be applied to the varying situations, would go contrary to the thrust of this approach, which is a refutation of the assumptions behind the multitudinist "how to" manuals for parochial life. Yet it is possible to observe and to sketch some ways in which "the Difference" might be expressed in varying instances. The poise of the parish, we have noted, stands it in good stead for the repersonalization of man, the liberation of God, and the realization of community. Four aspects in which these are observable are (in a summary borrowed from Alexander Miller), worship, teaching, discipline, vocation.

Worship. A glance at the church advertisements of metropolitan newspapers on any Saturday makes it clear that what is peddled in many congregations is a cut-to-order deity which can be adapted to man's purposes. No more need be said about the limitations of this pulpit huckstering. But much has happened recently in the concentration on worship that can be of avail here. The biggest boost has come from the architects who are building the new houses of worship. Instead of providing lecture halls for prancing preachers or borrowing outworn forms to evoke a false sense of security in worshipers, they—the better of them, that is—are asking basic questions. They begin at the beginning by striving to suggest the setting for the human-divine dialogue, the sacred converse. Reminiscence of the cave is in their buildings, enclosures of space which suggest temporary withdrawal for renewed resource. They imply "the Difference" between church and world. The tent is there too, to allow for the perfect parable: the People of God are on the march, and the roofs over the light, wide-open, airy churches overarching provide symbolic shelter. In a new approach to space and light, the attempt is to express "the Difference."

In the healthier forms of the liturgical movement which is making its way across the spectrum of Christendom a similar emphasis is finding its place. It is ironical that dilettante forms of the movement in Protestantism, concerned with beautifying or enriching worship, are borrowing the externals and overlays of Roman Catholic elements that are now being shed by the more informed and historically conscious Catholic liturgiologists. Where the liturgical re-evaluation is under way, whether in Congregationalism or Lutheranism or Anglicanism, there is a definable trend, and the ecumenical movement has supported this:

> What we are dealing with is the decisively important insight (which we call *liturgical realism* in opposition to every kind of nominalistic degeneration) that in the liturgy something is not merely spoken about, some inward possession is not simply "set forth," but something actually happens . . . the present moment [is] heavy with decision.[5]

Teaching. In the matter of teaching or doctrine, the stirrings at mid-twentieth century are most striking. We have all talked so much about a theological renascence that most of us probably believe it is here. No doubt such a renascence can be documented. In ministerial circles there are evidences of it that go beyond mere jargon or vogue. Yet if there is any warrant for our description of religion-in-general it would seem that the more profound insights of the recovery have had little telling effect on America as a whole. Following through on Thornton's typology, one would not expect it there, for the theology of which we are speaking here begins (though it does not end) with a stress on "the Difference." This is not immediately or massively attractive. It is to stir first of all in the Remnant.

Is not Protestantism still plagued by timidity when it comes to substantive expression? It is true that much of the American evangelical expression shied away from substance. American religion was Wesleyan for the most part; it stressed experience. But self-conscious Protestants have made giant strides in our own time in recovering the evangelical substance in Wesley's position, which included the theological capital he borrowed and assumed out of the historic Anglican line from which he did not wish to sever himself. If Christianity is a faith it is a faith in someone and something. It is not just a mood or a spirit of a climate or an atmosphere. So men within each Protestant tradition are affirming. Do we hear it enough from the pulpits or find it in the conversation of ministerial associations? Despite magnificent exceptions it would seem that the impasse of which we spoke earlier still remains.

Manuscripts which come over the transom to the office of a certain Protestant journal of preaching are valid documentation of this.[6] I am speaking of unsolicited offerings sent to a magazine which is associated in many readers' minds with an explicit theological interest; it is not known first of all as a "practical" paper for preachers. Hence we might expect that those who aspire to have their sermons appear in its pages would submit what they regard as their more serious substantive attempts. Yet the larger percentage of the sermons that are rejected represent well-meant moralisms which could have been presented in slightly less elevated terms by the men of good will on television. Seldom is the emphasis on classic Christian themes. Seldom does the weight fall on "Christ, the power of God and the wisdom of God." No doubt each preacher would aver that Christ is the hope for the persons he serves, the definitive revelation of God, the source and center of community. Yet moralistic sermons direct little attention to this center. Nor do moralisms allow for the preaching of God's Law.

Just how to go about preaching the Law in forms which are not capsuled so that the healing Gospel can really be effective would be difficult to say. But the positive moralities of much of our teaching and preaching seldom begin to fill the requirements. A great deal of our preaching is devoted to smoothing the Sameness instead of stressing "the Difference."

Discipline. So long as the borders of church and world are even visibly coextensive, as they are in the assumptions of religionized America, it is difficult to see where the Remnant concept can begin to come into play. At this point it is in order to recall our previous discussions about entrance requirements to the committed fellow-ship, integrity of church membership, instruction in the meaning of the faith, and even fencing the tables as the beginning of a strategy for recovery. The recovery of some sense of discipline is a promising sign in many denominations. It has nothing at all to do with legalism, and is decidedly inferior to integrity of church membership. But it may be one way of translating the hope of minister-ing to a distinct group initially *"because it is the only way to redeem all the Americans."* Discipline, in this sense, is not something which is imposed (as Law) but which attracts to a center (the Gospel).

Vocation. This would be a book in itself. Yet in a sense it can be no book at all because the varieties of response are so multiple and many-colored. How is "the Difference" expressed if the ex-ternals of life are to look the same (Again: "Good God! Is this really he? Why, he looks like an Inspector of Taxes!")? If the parochial Beatnik loses every vital tie with other people through superficial forms of rebellion he will probably not be able to make contact with a Remnant. If he deserts entirely the accepted world of the people he would serve, and grows the cult's beard and dons the conforming clothes of nonconformity he will probably be avoid-ing and escaping the real struggle with the world, the flesh, and the devil instead of witnessing against them or encountering them.

Let my refusal to spell out a program of vocation with "the Difference" not be interpreted as cowardice but rather as witness to the fact that it cannot be spelled out. The person who has known real community in the fellowship of worship, teaching, and discipline is becoming equipped for such vocation. It will be like a melody played by ear in the rhythms of twentieth-century life. In sacrifice and service, in the political arena and the day's work, in office and home and church, in Christian evangelism: here the Remnant has a broader opportunity for expression than in Thorn-ton's Rule of Prayer, though it may well take nourishment and impetus from prayer.

Having invested so much discursive energy in the parish, I should like to close this aspect of the argument by reference to cer-tain signs of change and of hope. There are countless evidences to draw upon, but we shall confine ourselves to three, corresponding to problems we have discussed in relation to "God, Man, and Community."

First, are there signs that theological trends are current in American parishes which would counteract the assumptions of religion-in-general in respect to the packaging of God? The easiest place to find them should be the historic churches most conscious of classic Christian witness; the most difficult place, the interdenominational or nondenominational community churches that have come to be associated in the popular mind with American suburbia. In the latter we would expect to find, and indeed do find, a concentration of many of the problems dealt with earlier in this book. But there are indications that more is being striven for among them.

The community church is most vulnerable in this type of discussion because it is most likely to conform or adapt itself to alien norms in religious life. It may take upon itself the form of the religionized community instead of the form of a servant. As such it enjoys tremendous good will, and the focus of attention in press and popular imagery is more likely to be on it than on the more remote denominational congregation. The community church grew out of the creative attempt to find a solution to the problem of over-churching the denominational competition. Particularly with the increase of mobility and suburban housing after World War II, it was found that a multitude of struggling little churches of similar background could often be superseded through comity or co-operation. The combined efforts and the implied nonaggression of a number of Protestant churches have been of great benefit.

For this asset many community churches have paid a high price. Their frequent attempts to become all things to all men theologically often result in their becoming little to any of them. When preaching is pitched to the patent needs and wants of the majority of the people, vital religious differences must be glossed over and the erosion of theological distinctions follows, to no one's profit. The resource of judgment and hope is spread so thin that in time of crisis the people are left with generalities. Nor does the theology of this type of church seem capable of generating ideas for a second generation. Reproduction is an enduring problem of hybrids! It is an unnecessary price many have paid; that they have paid it is an almost universal observation.

In theory such churches *can* become in microcosm what the ecumenical movement apparently is turning out to be: a reunitive reality on the highest common denominator. Is it not possible for community churches, often founded on a minimal creed and with a will to do what, at Amsterdam in 1948, the World Council of Churches declared itself as purposing: "We intend to stay together" —is it not possible for them to move into step two, as the larger movement is doing? The honeymoon is over in the ecumenical movement on its larger scale. Most of the partisans of getting-together are finding it necessary to examine the bases of coming together. Their task is not easy, but it is being undertaken in faith. Cannot community churches on the parochial level seek to express in today's terms the ancient consensus of the faith, the translation of God's tradition to man in Jesus Christ? Instead of taking this more painful and promising approach, they yield to the temptation to attract twentieth-century men on their own terms, and to begin —*and remain!*—on the level of lowest common denominator. Too often the result is a cut-to-size program based on suburban values which are seldom transcended.

Instead of risking embarrassment to specific churches by citing solutions which are not yet solutions, I shall point to two documentable instances where the recognition of need for change may bring about creative solution. The two examples are chosen because their character has been reported on by others, to the general satisfaction of the churches themselves. If in these two multitudinist parishes, which are so known for their nontheological and even antitheological approach, we can see some sense of awareness that more is asked we might put a finger on a most hopeful sign. Whereas some years ago these churches and their predecessors may have prided themselves on their desertion of theology, today they seem engrossed with the scramble to be numbered among those who share more enduring concerns. Call this social pressure or call it response to the Spirit; it is there. The churches which received national attention for their nontheological social dynamics have been hastening to revise the accepted picture.

The first is suburban Chicago's Glenview Community Church. This church, said *Time*,[7]

> throws its net in a businesslike way into [its] town with a campaign of mailing and follow-ups. Prospective parishioners are given a check list with eighty-five openings for adult participation. The church compels assent to no dogma; the emphasis is on participation. People often join "to meet new friends," or "for the children," or "to get into some activities," or because "with everything moving so fast, people need something to cling to."

But the Rev. Robert Edgar, pastor of the church, commented in retrospect:

> I have a suspicion that the great freedom our church has expressed over the sixteen years of its organization—when we said that there are no creeds in this church, that each of us may come in and find his own way as long as we believe in God and Christ and the Church and the Bible—has made it easier for us to accept the "religion of the American way" than the religion of Jesus Christ, to find our salvation in building up our own prestige and working out our self-sufficiency, which leads always to frustration, rather than finding our salvation in depending on God.

Is not this a moving "repentance" on the part of the man most responsible for what we could nominate as the technically most successful community church ministry in America? If he carries to its logical conclusion this complaint over what man hath wrought, the Rev. Mr. Edgar may be achieving something greater than any of his original dreams for Glenview envisioned.

Mr. Edgar is not alone in his defensiveness or sense of need for change. In its report on the Glenview church *Time* not only described its creative programming and multiple ministry but also presented some observations of its own: that this represents "a kind of Protestantism that is burgeoning in the suburban nondenominational churches all over the U.S. . . . dedicated to the new-time religion"; that Glenview has a "believe-as-you-like, worship-as-you-please" religion, in a "developmental-task-oriented" church. Immediately, however, the magazine protected itself against expected response. Declaring that "Glenview's ministers are sensitive to the criticism that their brand of religion is theologically thin," it quoted one minister of the church who pointed beyond the obvious social materialism of suburbia. But two weeks later all four of the church's ministers were quick to respond with a letter to the editor in which they dissociated themselves from non-theological country clubbery. And soon thereafter (on January 26, 1958) one of them preached a sermon extremely critical of *Time*'s analysis of Glenview Community Church as a "Protestantism hellbent . . . on fine fellowship, clubbiness and chumminess in a great chatty spiritual cafeteria." Said the minister: "Some of us think this a distortion of the truth."

The other example of the effort to scramble away from the suburban stereotype is the equally famed Park Forest (Chicago south suburban) United Protestant Church. This church was set upon a hill by William H. Whyte in *The Organization Man*. Because the book came to be regarded so widely as a dead-eye portrait of the new man of the 1950s its picture of religion in suburbia met equal acceptance. Most readers are probably familiar with Whyte's description of the church formed in a mass-produced suburb as a result of co-operation among members of many denominations. Its founders wish to refute the theological particularity that goes into most new churches and do so by forming a *useful* church. "We try not to offend anybody"; "Put all [our needs] together and you get what we're after—a sense of community. We pick out the more useful parts of the doctrine to that end."[8] While Whyte showed a curious reluctance to criticize in the church what he lampooned elsewhere, he did cite enough dissatisfied comments to raise some questions.

My own interview with the ministers of the Park Forest church and its newer counterparts suggested that, while they found much in Whyte's portrait congenial and helpful to their local promotion, they also resented his picture of their packaging of God to suit suburbia's social norms. A detailed sociological analysis which would not neglect the theological question would be in order here. However, out of the maze of topics discussed in two hours, I retained one clear and consistent impression: the ministers resent Whyte's description of their lack of theology. "I object strenuously to that part of the picture," said one who asked me to record his negation word for word. Now if these ideal type examples of normative adjustment to suburban norms resent this tag of suburban values, the implication is that *a theological norm which they are coming to respect is beginning to prevail.* And in that there must be hope.

The obverse of the packaging of God in our analysis has been the depersonalizing of man. Because of their strategic position, local churches are best poised to keep personal contact without the faintly patronizing personal touch. One reason for this is that the Christian parish is one of the few remaining noncommercial (let us hope) points of contact between person-in-need and person-who-wishes-to-help. The telephone in a parsonage may ring any hour of day or night and the minister is expected to serve free of charge and as much as the situation demands. He may be called to walk through the valley of the shadow of death hundreds of times in his own lifetime. He may know the exhilarating joy of participating in a look past death to destiny and glory. He is, if he is worth his salt, going to share with the anguished and the proud alike. And he is not to measure the worth of the person he serves, either for his potential value to an organization or for his past performance or for inherent worth. He dare ask only the question of need. Asking more than this is the one sin that most ministers still recognize as the sin which warrants defrocking. So long as this standard applies and keeps growing we do well to look to the parish, for all its frailties, with hope.

To some extent the limits to this person-to-person (or person-to-parson) tie become narrower as parish population increases. Statistics, group-think, committeeitis, multitudinism, and other easily diagnosable diseases appear on the scene. Men may become objects to be manipulated for institutional ends. In such a setting men are interchangeable. Christian fellowship is translated into a secular type of togetherness under Christian labels. And here in his first and last refuge, man is depersonalized. Participation in the life of the church as such includes the reaping of material or obvious psychic benefits—and the church contributes to illusory redemption. Involvement in the busy-busy activities of parish life becomes the measure of the ethical, and an inverted moralism results. In all this the moralistic message of many a pulpit is of no help. The gospel of individualism finds few outlets for expression in the new society, and in the organization of society the churches themselves provide as few.

If we are to look for signs of hope through the quest for the bad conscience and the promise of better things to come, where shall we seek? It would seem that the area of religious life where the institution is most tempted to depersonalize man to its own ends would be in the area of fund-raising. This is true for several reasons. First of all, churches now exist in a money world where exchange of services, barter, and the giving of nonmonetary gifts is severely limited as a means of advancing even a religious institution. The situation is different from that of the American past, when religion thrived on the hand-built church and the hand-pumped organ, on the load of wood and the butchered hog delivered to the parsonage. In a technical society men must be paid for professional tasks, for erecting churches and printing bulletins and magazines. Inflation affects the churches along with the rest of society.

Second, under the current American tax structure which is leveling the nation to what many would consider a mass middle class, other means of support have changed. Visit almost any mammoth temple erected in the 1880s or 1890s or early in this century and you will be told which man or family of wealth provided most of the money for it. Today few churches have endowments or patrons; they are not supported by "pillars." They have to rely on voluntary giving on the part of the many and are thrown upon their ingenuity to make ends meet in new ways.

Many have turned to fund-raising organizations, institutions which by their very nature are better equipped to manipulate the advertised-to man than to understand Christian motives for giving. Such firms must promise and prove successes—as indeed they do. Doctors bury their failures. What happens to fund-raising failures one never learns. When fund-raising firms first invaded the churches they usually presented simple, unvarnished business ethics and techniques with a bit of Christian terminological gloss. Many of them may still do so. One advertises that it handles people with "kid gloves"—a striking innovation for Cross-bearers!

But again, an observation concerning a change in approach is in order. It also reflects a change in situations. Today American Protestants are interested not only in success, but, here and there, they would like to see the proper motivation toward the proper goal involving the proper role of persons in the financial support of the churches. For this reason fund-raising campaigners are almost embarrassingly articulate theologically. They are under compulsion to prove that their methods are fully compatible with sacrificial motives and distinctly "Christian" standards of giving. Not only results but compatible means are promised in virtually every promotional brochure these organizations hand out.

Says one: "Essential depth often was lacking and . . . fundamental needs not always were served. . . . Fund-raising for a church is a program of stewardship—an act of faith—a reflection of Christian fellowship." Another reprints a testimonial from a bishop: "I am sure that the spiritual lives of many of our people have been enriched. . . ." Another: "The conduct of the campaign on a high spiritual plane has awakened all of our people." No doubt the proof of success along with this "something more" is a promotional asset. Nor need we believe everything we read. But the fact that a program in this sensitive area is necessarily advertised as compatible with human personal means, redemptive purposes, and Christian ethical norms brings hope.

The quest for community was aggravated by certain physical factors: population growth, mobility, decay; and also by certain psychic factors: anxiety, rootlessness, quest for security. The search was complicated by what we have termed panurbia as a symbol of the new way of thinking in America. Such a situation calls into serious question the pattern of church life which many have come to see as normative in our nation's development. I refer to fiercely democratic and individualistic congregationalism. Such a position seems inconsistent with the microcosmic or organismic conception of the parish in the Church as the Body of Christ. It is also unrealistic in America today. Are there signs of awakening to the necessity for a change in attitude toward hyper-congregationalism as a form of religious response in the human community?

Indeed there are. Old patterns of thought still nag and cause a lag. There is still nostalgia for the normal parish that will never be again. There are still those who await not only wistfully but with hope the day when the rat race will stop, when people will stop moving. And the insistent answer returns: This will never happen, given American mobility. Reluctance to meet this change of setting has caused many churches to delay revising their strategies. One urban church expert boasts that his denomination has the best rural church program in existence today—and, he adds with a glint in his eye, it uses this in the cities! His colleagues in other denominations will hardly wish to claim first place for their own complaints. Other congregations have been invaded by a sense of insecurity. They distort statistics and reconstruct population pyramids in disregard of the facts, with the intention of trying to rebuild their sense of mission where they are, in splendid isolation.

In every urban center a curious situation has resulted. During the years of suburban growth the churches of the inner city were often tempted to "live unto themselves." Misering their financial assets they did little in their jealousy to build up strong churches in new population centers. But suburbia somehow made its way, and it is the current zone of prosperity. The inner city in the midst of its attrition now often makes pleas which meet little response from the newly self-centered, burgeoning suburban churches. It will be interesting to watch step three, as urban renewal again attracts suburbanites to the heart of cities. Obviously the insecurities of such isolated developments hamper the Christian cause. Are there those who have begun to deal with this need for an interlocked sense of community in panurbia?

Ross Sanderson, one of the most respected among urban church experts, told the American Baptist Urban Convocation in Indianapolis in autumn 1957: "We must think urban. This we have not yet done with any adequacy." He continued:

If suburbia allows the inner city to stew in its own juice; if good solid neighborhoods ignore blighted urban areas; if exurbia turns up its nose in scorn at all but the bread-and-butter aspects of urban living; if centrally located churches have no regard for paganism in suburbia; if all our churches fail to realize, not merely intellectually but deep down in their inner conscious or even subconscious selves, *how interwoven are their fortunes,* how all of them are bound up together in one bundle of life, then are our emotional lives superficial, tawdry and sub-Christian. [Italics mine.][9]

It is disconcerting that American Protestantism has to learn from contemporary urban dynamics what it ought to have learned from Holy Scriptures; namely, the essential nature of the Church. But we should be pleased that it is learning at all.

The interwoven, interlocking character of the fortunes of local churches is a rediscovery that awaited a post-Protestant, post-congregationalist era in America. In a forgotten day of isolation and slow communications and relatively long-term residence, even episcopal churches took on what resembled a congregational character. Insistence on this archaic form of individualism is as pathetic now as is the accompanying scramble which claims theological justification exclusively for this pattern that once served America well. This form of congregationalism is part of the sectarianism which, according to Daniel Jenkins,

has many virtues, virtues of enthusiasm and fellowship and of emphasis on individual responsibility. . . . But among its many limitations is the very relevant one, that it has not shown itself capable of adapting itself for effective working in large-scale society, where political and economic organization becomes increasingly centralized. It flourishes best in a small community with a simple organization. . . .[10]

Today we are a large community with complex organization. From now on "we are all in this together." The day of tradition-oriented parish strength is gone. No one sits still long enough to let traditions grow. The congregational strength once derived from the charismatic character of a long-term prestige parson is ebbing. Hyper-congregationalism relied on pastoral dynasties, on financial tycoons who endowed churches, on "pillars" that stayed as pillars should. Today's mobility and flux no longer allow for any of these.

No doubt in such a situation episcopal and diocesan institutions have an advantage. But interwoven and interlocked congregationalism can combine their assets with advantages of its own. Here we may have to start anew, deal with beginnings. According to a reviewer of his *The Parish in Action,* the Archbishop of Cape Town "shows that it is possible to see the modern parish as an entity to be created rather than a survival to be preserved." This possibility is most certainly true in America, where the Victorian pattern is just as obsolete as elsewhere. When the new parish pattern is born, it will have to include a healthier measure of interlocking of finance, polities, and program as a strategic device. And, incidentally, as a new witness to the interlocking character of Christian lives.

If the parish with its personal possibilities in mass society can be relieved of many pressures that it is not proof against, it offers the most hopeful front for helping shape post-Protestant America into a newly Christian America. It must be informed from the theological centers as it is not at present. As denominations and parishes take upon themselves the form of a servant and in sacrificial living in conformity to Christ are transformed, we shall see the liberation of God, the repersonalization of man, the judgment of a proud society, and the quiet but more effective religious impulse unmoved by obsessive revivalizing. Such movement is likely to occur in the only way it ever has, within a creative minority and through—in a chastened, Biblical sense—the Remnant.

Nine

The Call for a Culture Ethic

A CULTURE ETHIC designed to help the churches in a time of cultural crisis must be based on an analysis of the cultural situation, an exploration of religious resources, and a certain ground of strategy. This preliminary study, which amounts largely to a call for such a culture ethic, has included some of these elements. It has analyzed the new shape of America's generalized religion. It has chosen as three lines of theological resource three Biblical pictures which seem to speak to our present discontents: the Biblical view of man in community; the revelation of God in the form of a servant; and the Remnant motif as an impulse for the sacred community. It has pursued largely one line of strategy among many possibilities, concentrating on the local parish unit and advocating for the churches a strategic retreat with a disciplined advance to follow.

Others who may agree in broad outline with the analysis presented here may seek different wells of resource or follow different avenues of strategy and recovery. But they will have to face certain problems attendant on any criticism of religion-in-general. The implied alternative, particularity of witness, seems to carry with it two liabilities. One, it seems to encourage and excite division and divisiveness at the very moment when American society seems sorely to need unifying agents. Two, the scandal of particularity seems to predestine its prophets to presumption and dogmatic arrogance.

158

Are these the necessary fruits of particularity? And if so, must we pay the price? The concerns of the generalizers, whether they be sentimentalists or hardheaded forgers of a democratic creed, seem valid indeed. But I am convinced that they can be met and countered. I believe that they must be met, and that clarity and distinctiveness of religious definition must be restored to Christian witness lest it come at the last to resemble the man in the street's idea of God as a "vague, oblong blur."

If we place today's shape of American religion against the picture of the past, we may learn some of the reasons for seeking a more profound theological basis for today's culture ethic. That will leave only the task of detailing ways to avoid the criticisms of the generalizers of religion. Despite frequent disclaimers, this book may have given the impression that the new shape of American religion is wholly new. On the contrary, it represents not breaches with the past but heightened continuities or accelerated tendencies. America has long been religiously pluralistic but today it is realizing its pluralism. Distinctive witness has long been eroding but today the process is more rapid. What is different, however, is that generalizing is now taking place not simply within the Protestant or the Christian community but within the religious community as a whole! If we go back to earlier moments in our history we may learn how to face the newer moment. In particular, we shall examine the strengths and shortcomings of a past solution.

Culture Christianity verged on culture religion at least twice before in the American past. An early instance was the comfortable relation between Virginian Anglicanism's or New England liberalism's way of life religion and the genteel version of the American Enlightenment. This relation matured in late colonial and early national times, to be jostled by the evangelical revivals and the Pietist-Methodist movements in their American cast. The circuit rider who visited every crossroads shouting "Behold, the Lamb of God which taketh away the sin of the world!" effectively put to rout Benjamin Franklin's aloof Supreme Being. The moment called for action and not for theory. And the Christian response of that time merits awe for the quality of its action though only limited respect for the theory accompanying the action. In that relatively uncomplicated hour of Protestant America's history it was not difficult to practice the positive part of church reform and to propagate the Gospel throughout the land. Little can be learned from that recovery for the forging of a culture ethic today.

A later instance was the formation of a culture Protestantism in the latter half of the nineteenth century. In many respects the parallels between that moment and our own are more obvious. The churches then basked in the glories of success. Many men and particularly Christian men were prosperous and they were reluctant to face social problems. Religion was an instrument of the economic and national cause. This was the Gilded Age and Andrew Carnegie preached the Gospel of Wealth. "Social Darwinism," a doctrine at once cruel and optimistic, prevailed in the business community and found echoes in the religious community. Intellectual assaults on the churches had led clergymen to various forms of capitulative adaptations. To John Fiske and Lyman Abbott evolution became God's way of doing things, while Henry Ward Beecher and other pulpit princes extolled the coextensiveness of God's Kingdom and Christian virtue and prosperity.

As Richard Hofstadter summarizes it, that moment carries curious resemblances to our picture of current America's compulsion to religiosity:

By the 1880's . . . religion had been forced to share its traditional authority with science, and American thought had been greatly secularized. Evolution had made its way into the churches themselves, and there remained not a single figure of outstanding proportions in Protestant theology who still ventured to dispute it. But evolution had been translated into divine purpose, and in the hands of skillful preachers religion was livened and refreshed by the infusion of an authoritative idea from the field of science. The ranks of the old foes soon could hardly be distinguished as they merged in common hostility to pessimism or skepticism about the promise of American life. The specter of atheism was no longer a menace, and surveys of the colleges where one would most expect to discover infidelity revealed how little there was.[1]

The moment has also caught the attention of Winthrop Hudson, who observes that the churches were the victims of their own success. The mission seemed to be accomplished. Discipline disappeared, faith lost its force, the churches lived at peace with the world, "lost their sense of a distinct and specific vocation in society and devoted their energies to social activities, humanitarian enterprises, and the building of costly edifices."[2] Francis P. Miller sees this as a "process which began with a culture molded by religious faith" and ended "with a religious faith molded by a national culture." It was a time for positive thinking and peace with a very confined God.

If we linger here for a moment it becomes clear that what had developed was a perverted version of a "Christ of Culture" situation, as H. Richard Niebuhr would call it. Niebuhr has spoken of a relationship in which a fundamental *agreement* between Christ and culture is uncritically assumed and accepted. Religion then has a strong Christian reminiscence, and it turns to the figure of Jesus of Nazareth, who appears as a hero of human culture and a culmination of human aspiration. "He confirms what is best in the past, and guides the process of civilization to its proper goal."[3] Representatives of this viewpoint feel "no great tension between church and world, the social laws and the Gospel, the workings of divine grace and human effort, the ethics of salvation and the ethics of social conservation or progress." In the culture-Christianity of the Gilded Age this viewpoint, which is capable of being sophisticated, was rendered in crass and primitive terms. And when it reached a nadir a new impulse appeared to counter it. In a brighter moment of American religious history the Social Gospel was born.

This is not the place to extol the virtues or analyze the shortcomings of a movement which is overcriticized in hindsight. America was in a social crisis and when the churches seemed least to care religious leaders suddenly brought them to care very much. The achievement can stand on its own merit; it does not need defenders. It produced penitents and bearers of the stigmata and workers for God, and that was enough for the time being. But built into the theoretical basis for the Social Gospel was the fatal weakness that makes it so vulnerable to later criticism. It turned out to be a "Christ of Culture" solution to a "Christ of Culture" problem and as such it could not cope with the depths of the human situation. The forces underlying the social crisis could not so easily be exorcized as Shailer Mathews and Walter Rauschenbusch and George Herron and Washington Gladden seemed to think.

Rauschenbusch was the most realistic of them all, and by the time his *A Theology for the Social Gospel* appeared (1917) he had undertaken considerable work of revision. Hudson does well to see him as "a lonely prophet" even among the prophets. But Rauschenbusch's characteristic term, "Christianizing" the social order, carried the seeds of return to the generalizing of Christianity it sought to counter. He was the Christ-centered evangelist that he insisted he was, but his view of divine immanence in social structures, of the interpenetration of Christ and culture, of a transformed culture often led him to what he stormed against in others: eulogy of culture and the merging of secular and sacred. For this function, Rauschenbusch insisted, one dare not become too precise theologically: "safety lies in vagueness," which can rally more parties to single causes.

This is the point at which the somewhat elusive concept of "Christianizing" entered. The family, the church, and education were relatively Christianized. The political and economic orders must follow. The task was great; but Rauschenbusch would "rather meet God in a dream than not meet him at all." And his dream of God had to become so all-inclusive that it broke Rauschenbusch's own attempt at synthesis. Particularity's cutting edge was dulled so that at many points Rauschenbusch, representing the Social Gospel at its best, seems to veer toward sanctified secularity as normative Christian witness.

The Social Gospel came into bad times in its own time because it was not really a Gospel; it was an ethic and it dealt first of all with Law. Where it played with Gospel it tended to merge with the American democratic creed. And in a slightly later day, with the shattering effects of World War I, the illusory solution of social problems in the 1920s, and the depression of the 1930s, many of the "Social" props were also pulled away. Even the assets of the Social Gospel's position are not available nationally today. Rauschenbusch and his fellows could still assume that Christianity, not religion in general, was the factor to reckon with in national life. But today anyone who shares the Social Gospel's approach must speak of a "Religion of Culture" and of "Religionizing" the social order. If distinctive witness was blurred in Social Gospel Protestantism, it is in greater danger in Positive Thinking Protestantism.

So in place of a Social Gospel, which assumes too much, a

culture ethic is called for today. It might have various theoretical justifications. In Niebuhr's terms, it may begin with "Christ above Culture" or "Christ Transforming Culture" or "Christ and Culture in Paradox." But religious America does not offer the option of "Christ of Culture"—unless the "Christ" designates something hazy or devoid of content and specific reference. Such a culture ethic is likely to see that the contact between church and society is made not through Gospel but first of all through Law, through the Church's agency as custodian of God's Law as it apprehends His revelation.

Such an ethic, concerned as it is with preserving distinctive Christian witness, is, we have said, in danger of appearing as a destructive, divisive, and thus annihilating force in an America that is sorely in need of unifying forces. Is it not a fact that if Protestants seek to extricate themselves from a religion which would merge them with a culture there is some risk in this respect? Will there not be new holy wars if we begin once again to contend for the faith not because we believe it to be useful but because we believe it to be true? The record of Christian history certainly gives reason for uneasiness on this score. Ugly passions have been roused in defense of a particular witness; blood has been let in defense of truth; nowhere does *hybris* rear its head higher than when parties claim an exclusive hold on "the pure doctrine."

In America we must coexist. Are we not better off muddling through and leaving to each generation a lesser legacy of faith's content so that each may share more of faith's forms? The variety and multiplicity of denominations in this country remains bewildering. Assertions of particularity will certainly jangle as we hear them renewed from Roman Catholic, Jewish, Protestant, Orthodox, Anglican, Lutheran, and Ethical Cultural sources. Must we entertain the claims of all 258 denominations in the *Yearbook of American Churches*—of

> Church of God (Cleveland, Tenn.)
> Church of God (Anderson, Ind.)
> Church of God (Seventh Day)
> The (Original) Church of God, Inc.
> The Church of God
> The Church of God (Seventh Day), Denver, Colo.
> The Church of God of Prophecy

Evangelistic Church of God
Church of God and Saints of Christ
Church of God in Christ

and even the "House of God, Which is the Church of the Living God, the Pillar and the Ground of the Truth, Inc."? (It too is registered with 119 churches!) What will happen to the American consensus and national good will?

These are real concerns, and they will test the religious character of the religious organizations. But the threat can be exaggerated. There are certain safeguards against it. First, most of Protestantism falls into nine or ten largely congenial denominational families busy finding unity among one another as they find unity in Christ in the ecumenical movement. My devotion to the ecumenical cause and my hopes for it are so ardent that I would rather withdraw my whole argument than to see it undercutting the dream of Christian unity. But it is a dream anchored in the hope that if we "hold to Christ, and for the rest be totally uncommitted," we will learn to enhance and share our particular histories "that we may all be one." Not only is it possible to hold the particular vision with greater clarity while learning new attitudes toward others within the ecumenical movement: the striking fact is that fundamentalists and "neo-evangelicals" in their conclaves and confraternities are in quest of unities among the intransigents. Even if their motive seems often merely antiecumenicalism, they are proving that unities exist which they had not previously known.

A second safeguard resides in the nature of Biblical religion as it makes its way into the traditions that emerge from it: the power of love can cross lines of ideological difference between neighbors. Men can love each other as persons even when personhood is made up to a large extent of ideas held by someone with whom they cannot agree.

It is to a third line of argument that we must turn, however, if we wish to see the potential of renewal in a time of blurred witness. In an earlier chapter I remarked on the seemingly paradoxical increase of religious tension at a time when distinctiveness of vision was disappearing.

In the 1950s, just when millions of Americans were preaching the doctrine that it made no difference what one believed provided one did believe, so that there was less reason for the existence of separate churches, there was a proportionate increase in interreligious tensions. Not for decades had the specter of mistrust loomed up so frequently between Protestant and Catholic; synagogues were bombed; national leaders grew uneasy whenever religious issues were introduced. But this only seems to be a paradox; it represents activity flowing out of ignorance. Men mistrust what they do not know and what they cannot understand.

Here, another example from the American past is illuminating. The anti-Catholic and anti-Continental Nativist and Know-Nothing movements of a century ago represent the blackest pages in America's Protestant history. If we ask why Protestant mistrust and persecution prevailed at that moment, the answer seems to be that people were afraid of the unknown; they reacted in anxiety. If a man sees an object of definable size and force coming toward him he can put a creative fear to work and get out of its way. If the object is of indeterminate size and force and nature, his responses are diffuse and disproportionate. He is anxious, and his responsive behavior will be erratic.

Apply this to the current scene. Protestants and Catholics looking at each other's histories and careers as power blocs have good cause to fear each other. But this fear can issue in creative action. They can seek understanding and agreement. They can find patterns of coexistence and seek redress in the larger political community. They can respect and love one another as persons. They can increase this respect as they explore their own deeper religious resources and recognize integrity of commitment. But Protestants and Catholics who lose the particularity of their witness must find alien grounds of justification for their separate existence. They become *only* power blocs or mass movements, with all the consequent liabilities. In place of fear there is anxiety. In place of encounter across conference tables there is encounter across back-alley fences and in smoke-filled corridors and on the pages of yellow journals, and on battlefields where both "sides" have kicked up the dust so that they cannot see.

Particular witness, then, need be emotionally divisive only if men choose to make it so. Here each group has its own temptations. My remarks, however, are directed only to Protestantism with the peculiar resources of understanding a vision beyond its own. At the base of most of the problems in the new shape of American religion is that morally and intellectually debilitating relativism which has produced the packaged God, the personless man, and the blurred community. If particularity is recovered, will this not also imply the resurrection of arrogant absolutisms?

I submit that it need not. The Protestant groups that are convinced that they have an absolute hold on absolute truth are usually realistic enough to recognize their minority and sectarian status, and so there is little reason for concern from them. This may be the problems of what many patronizingly refer to as "the sects" but it is so little the problem of mainstream Protestantism that we can with confidence deal with the alternative. The alternative is the tendency to absolutize another principle: that we have only a relative hold on relative truth; that we slip and slide on greased skillets; that we can ultimately know nothing and love nothing and believe nothing to be true except the principle that one must have faith in faith.

Relativism is the position which sophisticates the "after all we are in different boats heading for the same shore" principle to the point where it hardly makes any difference in which boat we are. I am not saying that an implied universalism with its belief that ultimately the love of God will overcome the wrath and justice of God is a base motive. It may proceed from the deepest resources of love and may prove somehow to be "true." But when Protestant Christianity becomes the propagandizer of such a vision it is arrogating to itself something which is God's own province to declare, and which is not declared in the revelation that gives birth to the Christian faith and its mission. "Neither is there salvation in any other: for there is none other name under heaven given among men, whereby we must be saved." Religion-in-general fuses this name with all others, and this fusion dulls the impetus of Christian missionary endeavor.

The temptation then is to go to the opposite extreme and to suggest that what America needs today is a new competition of absolutistic claims. People want security, and the churches would do well to give them a rock to stand on, some sort of creed which appropriates a cloak of infallibility for its professors. So runs the advice. Thus the pure doctrine becomes something instrumental, something that justifies the claims of a human religious organization just as social activities or eleemosynary functions justify other organizations. The end result is simply another reduction or packaging of God.

There are other alternatives. They begin with the proclamation of what is the truth *for us* and our community, presented as an option for the faith and hope of the world. Such a proclamation begins with "confession" and not with "apology," to use H. Richard Niebuhr's distinction.[4]

As we begin with revelation only because we are forced to do so by our limited standpoint in history and faith so we can proceed only by stating in simple, confessional form what has happened to us in our community, how we came to believe, how we reason about things and what we see from our point of view.

Religious response to revelation is made quite as much in a confession of sin as in a confession of faith and a theology which recognizes that it cannot speak about the content of revelation without accepting the standpoint of faith must also understand that it cannot deal with its object save as sinners' rather than saints' theology.

This approach is of honored lineage. It has its confessional birth in the New Testament:

That which was from the beginning, which we have heard, which we have seen with our eyes, which we have looked upon and touched with our hands, concerning the word of life—the life was made manifest, and we saw it, and testify to it, and proclaim to you the eternal life which was with the Father and was made manifest to us—that which we have seen and heard we proclaim also to you, so that you may have fellowship with us; and our fellowship is with the Father and with his Son Jesus Christ. And we are writing this that our joy may be complete. [I John 1:1–4]

That the proclamation can be cast in humility and hope is also clear from St. Paul's testament in the most famous passage of Scripture he wrote, remembered as I Corinthians 13:

. . . as for prophecy, it will pass away; as for tongues, they will cease; as for knowledge, it will pass away. For our knowledge is imperfect and our prophecy is imperfect; but when the perfect comes, the imperfect will pass away. . . . now we see in a mirror dimly, but then face to face. Now I know in part; then I shall understand fully, even as I have been understood.

In place of dissipating relativism there can be witness to truth tempered by recognition of the incompleteness of all human vision.

The German translates it: our knowledge is *Stückwerk,* it is piece-work and imperfect. But we do have knowledge; this is what religion-in-general's relativizing position forgets.

The Reformation, despite the systematizing arrogance to which it was often tempted and of which it often became captive in its second generation, also provides resources on which its heirs can draw. This is the point of Luther's "theology of the cross" as opposed to the "theology of glory." The theology of the cross looks at the "hind parts of God"; it is empirical, operating with what it can know and love: the wounds of Christ. As such it refuses to peer into the heavenly majesty and to claim God's own thoughts and ways captive of the vision. Even more patent as a ground for tolerance (so weak a word!) without loss of confessional rigor was the viewpoint of many a Puritan, particularly the sectarians. Thus John Saltmarsh in his *Smoke in the Temple* (1646): "Let us not assume any power of infallibility to each other; . . . for another's evidence is as dark to me as mine to him . . . till the Lord enlighten us both for discerning alike." But a sentimentalizing Protestantism forgets that it *does* have evidence and *does* have enlightening, and that it must be faithful to this heavenly vision and to its highest convictions without first being dissolved in the thin waters of generalized everything-true-nothing-true religion.

An emergent culture ethic, then, must with its analysis, resource, and strategy develop a spirit which will lead neither to divisiveness nor to arrogance. It will need other dimensions which this preliminary study cannot provide. In discussing the new shape of *American* religion we have been somewhat provincial, failing to see the moment against the background of world revolution. Reference to the world scene and the universal aspects of the Christian ecumenical movement will bring depth to such an ethic: for the American cultural situation is in many respects isolated, and this insular prospect may limit our grasp of resources for recovery. The "younger churches" and the mission fields can introduce a note of realism from nations where the Christian religion is not experiencing prosperity and success.

As this ethic is forged in seminaries and universities, in conference rooms and local churches and private closets, it will make its way inspired by confidence and urgency. Its confidence arises from its call to faith: "For I am sure that neither death, nor life, nor angels, nor principalities, nor things present, nor things to come, nor powers, nor height, nor depth, nor anything else in all creation, will be able to separate us from the love of God in Christ Jesus our Lord." Its urgency derives from its openness to the future and its recall of the past, across which a haunting voice is still heard, "When the Son of man cometh, shall he find faith on the earth?"

Notes

Chapter One. *The Revival of Interest in Religion*

1. (New York: Association Press, 1958), p. 19.
2. Emerson W. Harris, "Our Popular Religious Narcissism," in *The Churchman,* August 1957, p. 6.
3. See especially *Errand into the Wilderness* (Cambridge: Harvard University Press, 1956), Chaps. III, VI, VII; *The Great Awakening in New England* (New York: Harper, 1957), p. 139; *Revivalism and Social Reform* (Nashville: Abingdon, 1957), pp. 93 f.
4. C. Wright Mills, "A Pagan Sermon to the Christian Clergy," *The Nation,* March 8, 1958, p. 200.
5. In *The Genius of American Politics* (Chicago: University of Chicago, 1953), p. 148.

Chapter Two. *The God of Religion-in-General*

1. In *Religion and the Free Society* (New York: Fund for the Republic, 1958), pp. 5 ff.
2. Quoted in Frederick K. Wentz, *The Times Test the Church* (Philadelphia: Muhlenberg, 1956), p. 132.
3. (New York: Harper, 1935), pp. 17, 24 f.
4. (New York: Vintage, 1956), p. xii.
5. See the Report in *The Nation,* March 8, 1958, by Harvey Swodos.
6. See *The Christian Century,* "The New Look in American Piety," November 17, 1954, and the extension of this subject in Eckardt's book. (See note 1, Chap. I.)
7. In *The Fabulous Future: America in 1980* (New York: Dutton, 1956), pp. 194, 198 f.
8. *Op. cit.,* pp. 55, 63.

Chapter Three. *Man in Religionized America*

1. (New York: McGraw-Hill, 1958), unpaged.

2. Much of this summary is from Daniel Bell's perceptive critique, "The Theory of Mass Society," in *Commentary,* July 1956.

3. In *Religion in America,* edited by John Cogley (New York: Meridian, 1958), pp. 194 f.

4. In *Frontiers in American Catholicism* (New York: Macmillan, 1957), pp. 4, 17, 21.

5. Reprinted in *Religious Education* (New York: The Religious Education Association, March–April, 1958), p. 110.

6. "The Organization and the Individual," in *Christianity and Crisis,* June 24, 1957, pp. 83 ff.

7. In *What the Christian Hopes for in Society,* edited by Reinhold Niebuhr (New York: Association, 1957), pp. 75–76.

8. *His,* November 1958, pp. 30 ff.

9. "Theology and Freedom," in *The Churchman,* September 1958, pp. 6–7.

10. (New York: Harper, 1957), p. 91.

Chapter Four. *America's Real Religion: An Attitude*

1. In *Patterns of Faith in America Today* (New York: Harper, 1957), p. 170.

2. In *A Guide to the Religions of America* (New York: Simon & Schuster, 1955) p. 169.

3. "Charles Fleischer's Religion of Democracy," in *Commentary,* June 1954, p. 557.

4. Excerpts from *Man's Vast Future* (New York: Farrar, Strauss and Young, 1951). The full scope of Davies' thought is presented in *The Mind and Faith of A. Powell Davies* (New York: Doubleday, 1959).

5. Most of Mrs. Meyer's words reproduced here are from a speech to the American Unitarian Association in 1954. See also "The Clerical Challenge to the Schools," in *Atlantic,* March 1952, and comment in *The Commonweal,* June 4, 1954.

6. See all of Chap. XIV in J. Paul Williams, *What Americans Believe and How They Worship* (New York: Harper, 1952).

7. *Reflections on America* (New York: Scribner's, 1958), pp. 186–88.

Chapter Five. *The Setting for the Future: Panurbia*

1. *The New Ordeal of Christianity* (New York: Association, 1957), p. 110.

2. *Op. cit.,* p. xi.

3. See C. Wright Mills, *White Collar* (New York: Oxford Galaxy edition), pp. xiii–xiv.

4. Mark Rich has summarized the developments in *The Rural Church Movement*. (Columbia, Mo.: Juniper Knoll, 1957). See also *Pulpit Digest*, July 1957, pp. 5 ff.

5. In the excerpt from "Epitaph for Dixie," in *Life*, November 4, 1957, p. 144.

6. (Princeton: Princeton University Press, 1958). See especially Chaps. II, 4 and IV, 9.

7. Anthony Winthrop, Jr., "The Crab-Grass Roots of Suburbia," in *The New Republic*, February 11, 1957, pp. 17 ff.

8. *The Christian Century*, September 28, 1955.

Chapter Six. *Signposts to Theological Resources*

1. Translated by A. S. Todd (Philadelphia: Westminster, 1957), pp. 161 ff.

2. *A Theological Word Book of the Bible*, edited by Alan Richardson (New York: Macmillan, 1951), p. 82.

3. "Fellowship and/or Freedom," in *The Christian Century*, April 17, 1957, pp. 490 ff.

4. *The Man in the Mirror* (New York: Doubleday, 1958), pp. 159 ff.

5. (New York: Harper, 1953), Chap. XI and especially p. 258.

6. Quoted by Miller, *op. cit.*, p. 159.

7. S. Kierkegaard, *Fear and Trembling* (New York: Oxford University Press, 1946), p. 49.

Chapter Seven. *The Poise of the Parish*

1. Michael Furlong in *The Commonweal*, September 20, 1957, in reference to Father J. B. Gremillion's *Journal of a Southern Pastor*.

2. Quoted by Tom Allan, *The Face of My Parish* (New York: Harper, n. d.), p. 67.

3. *Protestant and Catholic* (Boston: Beacon, 1957), p. 126.

4. Erik Routley, *The Gift of Conversion* (Philadelphia: Muhlenberg, 1958), pp. 136–37.

Chapter Eight. *The Practice of the Parish*

1. By Guido Merkens (St. Louis: Concordia, 1958). More unilaterally programmatic is Willard Pleuthner's *More Power for Your Church: Building Up Your Congregation* (New York: Farrar, Strauss and Cudahy, 1959).

2. *The Purpose of the Church and Its Ministry* (New York: Harper, 1956), Chap. 2, III.

3. (London: S.P.C.K., 1956), Chaps. 4, 5, 21. The whole argument of the book is under review here. See especially pp. 73, 158.

4. *The Reporter*, January 13, 1955.

5. "Liturgy as Decision" by Wilhelm Stoehlin, in *The Lutheran World Review*, October, 1949, pp. 78 ff.

6. *The Pulpit,* published by the Christian Century Foundation. I do not wish to imply that all rejected sermons are "moralistic" or that all printed ones are not!

7. See Stanley J. Rowland, Jr., *Land in Search of God,* pp. 72 f., 80, and *Time,* January 27, 1958, p. 52.

8. See Chap. 27 of *The Organization Man* (New York: Simon and Schuster, 1956).

9. From a Baptist News Service release, October 25, 1957.

10. *Europe and America: Their Contributions to the World Church* (Philadelphia: Westminster, 1951), p. 23.

Chapter Nine. *The Call for a Culture Ethic*

1. *Social Darwinism in American Thought* (Boston: Beacon, 1955), p. 30.

2. *Op. cit.,* pp. 201 f.

3. H. Richard Niebuhr, *Christ and Culture* (New York: Harper, 1951), p. 41.

4. H. Richard Niebuhr, *The Meaning of Revelation* (New York: Macmillan, 1941), pp. 40–41.

Index

Abbott, Lyman, 160
Adams, Samuel, 80
American Baptist Urban Convocation, 155
American Character, The, 35
American Economic Association, 95
American Scholar, 47
American Way of Life, 32, 59
Anglicans, Anglicanism, 68, 70, 115, 139, 145 f., 159, 163
anthropological question, 109 ff.
Antonines, Antonine Rome, 21, 70
Apostles' Creed, 35 f.
Arminians, Arminianism, 8, 24, 27 f., 42 f., 54 ff., 63 f., 72, 95
Arminius, Jakob, 55
Ashmore, Harry, 97
Athenians, 20
Atonement, 115
Attorney-General, 61
Augustine, 106, 120
Aulén, Gustav, 32

Baird, Robert, 72
Baptists, 42
Barth, Karl, 65, 112
Beckett, Samuel, 106
Beecher, Edward, 24
Beecher, Henry Ward, 160
Beecher, Lyman, 8
Bell, Daniel, 51
Bellarmine, 56
Bensman, Joseph, 97
Bergson, Henri, 122

Berryman, John, 60
Bible Belt, x
Biblical theology, 29 f., 111
Black, John D., 95
Blake, Eugene Carson, 77
Body of Christ, 112, 123
Boorstin, Daniel, 29
Boyd, Malcolm, 105
Brainstorming, 38 f.
Brogan, Daniel W., 29, 35, 94, 98
Bryan, William Jennings, 107
Buber, Martin, 29, 53
Buddhism, 35, 48

Calvin, Calvinism, 8, 19, 23, 28, 33 f., 42, 48, 54 f., 57, 72
Camus, Albert, 87
Carnegie, Andrew, 160
Carroll family, 3
Cartwright, Peter, 8
Christ and Adam, 65
Christian Action, 19
Christian Century, The, x, 26, 64, 73, 130 f.
Christianity and Crisis, 20, 26
"Christianizing," 162
"Christ of Culture," 161 f.
Christology, 114 ff.
Church, doctrine of, 117 ff.
Church Federation of Chicago, 13
Church of England, 4
Church[es] of God, 163
Civil War, 12

175

Golden, Harry, 13
Gospel of Wealth, 160
Graham, Billy, 12 f., 21 ff., 39, 43,
  64, 107 f., 132
*Great Tradition of the American
  Churches, The*, 118
*Guide to the Religions of America,
  A*, 77

Handlin, Oscar, 72
Harper's, 13
Harris, Emerson W., 20
Harvard, 13
Hawthorne, Nathaniel, 43
Herberg, Will, 54, 59, 70, 73, 101
Herron, George, 161
Higginson, Francis, 108
Hinduism, 104
His, 64
Hitler, Adolf, 51
Hofstadter, Richard, 160
Holy Spirit, 36 f., 129
Hudson, Winthrop, 118, 160, 162
humanism, 76 ff.
Hutchinson, Paul, 15, 73, 93 f.
Huxley, Julian, 13

Incarnation, 37, 56, 115, 125
inner city, 102 ff.
International Press Institute, 37
Interurbia, 104
Islam, 104

Jacobs' study, 61
James, Henry, 43
James, William, 38
Jaspers, Karl, 49
Jefferson, Thomas, 68 f., 79 f., 84
Jenkins, Daniel, 156
Jesus, 19, 21 f., 27, 35 f., 57, 64, 85,
  102, 109, 112 ff., 114 ff., 128,
  139 ff., 146, 150, 161, 167, 169
John XXIII, Pope, 74

Judaism, 2 ff., 10, 14, 26, 29, 32, 48,
  67, 69 ff., 87, 89, 101, 102 f., 163

Keats, John, 99
Khrushchev, Nikita, 16
Kierkegaard, Soren, 120
Kirkland, William, ix, 113 f.
Know-Nothing, 165
Knox, John, 19
Köhler, Ludwig, 111 ff.
koinonia, 112 ff.

Lewis, C. S., 11, 36
Liebman, Joshua Loth, 18, 27
Lincoln, Abraham, x, 43, 76, 80
Living Church, The, 65
Locke, John, 80
Loew, Cornelius, 119
Look, 77
Luce, Henry, 17, 41
Luther, Martin, 66, 119, 168
Lutheranism, 26, 42, 57, 145, 163

Madison Avenue, 17
Madison, James, 68
Madison Square Garden, 25
man, doctrine of, 19 f.
Mann, Arthur, 78, 85
Mannheim, 49
Man's Vast Future, 79
Maori tribes, 52
Mao Tse Tung, 16
Maritain, Jacques, 29, 78, 85
Marshall, Peter, 12, 20
Mary, 35
Massachusetts Institute of Technology, 78
Mass evangelism, 21 ff.
mass society, 49 ff.
Mathews, Shailer, 161
McCall's, 113
McCarthyism, 12
McLoughlin, William, 64
McPartland, John, 98

O

J

DATE DUE

JUN 1 5 1986	